WEST AFRICA, ISLAM, AND THE ARAB WORLD

West Africa, Islam, and the Arab World

Studies in Honor of Basil Davidson

John Hunwick

Markus Wiener Publishers
Princeton

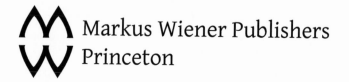

For information write to:
Markus Wiener Publishers
231 Nassau Street, Princeton, NJ 08542
www.markuswiener.com

Front cover design by Noah Wiener
Book design by Wangden Kelsang

Library of Congress Cataloging-in-Publication Data

Hunwick, John O.
West Africa, Islam, and the Arab world : studies in honor of Basil Davidson / John Hunwick.
p. cm.
Includes bibliographical references and index.
ISBN-13: 978-1-55876-398-2 (hardcover : alk. paper)
ISBN-10: 1-55876-398-8 (hardcover : alk. paper)
1. Africa, West--Civilization. 2. Islam--Africa, West--History. 3. Africa, West--Religion. 4. Africa, West--Relations--Arab countries. 5. Arab countries--Relations--Africa, West. 6. Arabic language--Africa, West--History. 7. Africa, West--Ethnic relations. 8. Manuscripts, Arabic. I. Title. DT474.H865 2006
305.6'970966--dc22

2006029944

ISBN-13: 978-1-55876-399-9 (paperback)
ISBN-10: 1-55876-399-6 (paperback)

Printed in the United States of America on acid-free paper.

Contents

Preface

It is a pleasure to be able to present these studies to Basil Davidson, who has written many books on Africa and its history. Beginning his career as a journalist, his writing has been easily and pleasantly readable, though he has always read the works of academic historians, and hence given accurate approach to African history in his writings. Biographical and bibliographical information on him is to be found in Section IV of this book.

I am also happy to personally have a David-son—my son David, a Macintosh computer expert, who has helped me much with formatting this book. I am also happy to be writing a book that will be useful to two of my other descendants who have interests similar to mine: my son Joseph—often in Timbuktu, and often called there Yūsuf al-Tinbuktī; and my granddaughter Jessica, who, at age 14, has already begun to learn the Arabic language and read the Qur"ān, being also interested in West Africa.

My writings in this book reflect much of the research I have done over the past half century, both on West Africa—where I also taught in universities in Nigeria and Ghana—and on Islam and Arabic writings, which were the principal matters of my original academic study.

These studies are pricipally based on talks that I have given at conferences and at universities, but have revised and updated to reflect new research and new conceptions. I hope that this book will be a useful resource for additional study by former graduate students of mine and any other future students of Islam and Africa.

John Hunwick
Emeritus Director
Institute for the Study of Islamic Thought in Africa
February 2006

GLOSSARY

All words are Arabic, except some indicated as Hausa

Alƙali [Hausa]	(Arabic: *al-qāḍī*) Islamic judge
Amır	Prince
Baraka	Blessing
Basasa [Hausa]	Civil war
Bilād al-sūdan	"Land of the Blacks", i.e. sub-Saharan Africa
Dīnār	Gold coin
Fāsī	Belonging to Fez (*Fās*)
Fatwā	Opinion document of Islamic ruling on a matter
Fiqh	Islamic jurisprudence
Faqīh	Muslim jurist
Galadima [Hausa]	Official
Gaisuwa [Hausa]	Tribute
Ḥadīth	Saying of the Prophet Muḥammad
[al-]Ḥaramayn	Two holy places: Mecca and Madīna.
Ḥarāṭīn	Black Saharan groups
Hijra	Emigration
ʿĪd	Religious festival
Jihād	Islamic "holy" war
Juzʾ	Part or section
Khalīfa	Caliph: president of the Islamic community
Madh'hab	Islamic law school
Malam [Hausa], p. *malamai*	(Arabic: *muʿallim*) Scholar, teacher
Mithqāl	Cash weight amount [of gold] = 0.15 oz.
Nawāzil	Legal actions
Nisba	Relationship
Sharīʿa	Sunni Islamic law
Risāla	Letter, written report
Sāḥil	Coast = edge of the Sahara (Sahel)
Sharīf	Nobleman
Shaykh	Senior scholar, or Islamic leader
Sūdān	Black people (pl. of *aswad*)
Ṭarīqa	Sufi brotherhood
Waqf	A religious endowment
Zāwiya	Prayer room, small mosque

Part I

West Africa

Chapter One

Introduction to West Africa[1]

(i) Climate, Languages and Peoples

West Africa is to be defined as the area south of the Sahara between the Atlantic coast in the west and Lake Chad with the highlands to the south of it in the present-day Republic of Cameroon. The land in the southern area of West Africa towards the Atlantic Ocean is largely of tropical forest, and then northwards of it is a zone of pasture and partial forest, and then northwards of it is a zone known as the Sahel (from the Arabic word *sāḥil* for 'coast'), with semi-sandy soil and some bushes (but rarely any trees), leading into the Saharan region, which has a surface of sand and some rocks, with little growth of anything, except small bushes in in some places, and occasionally, if heavy rain ever falls, some pasture which camels can feed on.

The most southerly regions get quite heavy rainfall every year from February or March to October or November, with temperatures mainly in the eighties Fahrenheit. The farther north one gets, a smaller amount of rain falls over a shorter period of the year. Occasionally there are unexpected rainfalls, even as far north as Timbuktu, at the Saharan edge of the Sahel. Once in the late twentieth century, when I was in Timbuktu, rain fell one day in January—evidently an extension of the Mediterranean winter rain, coming across the Sahara and also watering oases. Again, in August 1999, the rainfall was so great one day that some roads in the south of the city had floods, and one area there just became a lake; while elsewhere some adobe-built houses had roof collapses, and some had rainwater penetrate into them—damaging manuscripts in some houses. In March, during the 'Ḥarmattan' season (December-February), Timbuktu gets wind from the north, bringing with it Saharan sand, even blowing as far south as Bamako, though by there with less, or no, sand in it.

The different climates obviously allow different growths, though one form or another of grass is found almost everywhere. In the regions closer to the coast, and hence warmer and with greater rainfall, agriculture often produces corn, yams, bananas, mangoes, melons, oranges, and many other fruits and vegetables. Rice is often grown by the banks of the river Niger, when areas are flooded, just as that huge river also produces large quantities of fish.

West Africans speak a large number of languages belonging to three major families: Niger-Congo, Nilo-Saharan, and Afro-Asiatic. This latter family—of which the widely-spoken Hausa is a member—also has in it some languages primarily belonging to the Middle East, such as Ancient Egyptian, Hebrew, and Arabic In fact, Arabic is also spoken in some parts of the Sahelian region of West Africa, and has been extensively used as a literary language for Muslims. Niger-Congo is the family containing the majority of languages spoken in West Africa, especially in the more tropical regions; e.g. Yoruba, Igbo, Akan, Ewe, and Mossi. Nilo-Saharan is a much smaller family, spoken only on the edges of the Sahara—by groups that migrated southwards when the Sahara became a completely desert zone by around 2,000 B.C.; Songhay is probably one such language, though the French linguist Nicolai more recently gave other views of it; notably defining it as a Tamasheq creole.[2]

Almost all of West Africa came under European—British or French—colonial rule from the late nineteenth century until the mid-twentieth century, with independence of most of the countries occurring around 1960. Portugual also took over one small area, in 1879, now known as Guinea-Bissau. The United States of America took over in 1822 an area that was later known as Liberia, after freed Afro-American slaves retired there, and in 1847 Liberia declared independence and took control of the indigenous population. After independence, some ex-colonial states changed their names: Soudan français became Mali immediately, and Gold Coast became Ghana, and much later Haute-Volta (or Upper Volta) became Burkina Faso, and Dahomey became Bénin. Other West African countries, that retained their names after independence, include: Senegal, Gambia, Sierra Leone, Côte d'Ivoire, Togo, Niger, Nigeria, and Cameroon.

Each country has a large number of ethnic groups, speaking different languages, and originally having different religious beliefs and practices. Former colonial countries still use either English or French as their "official" languages, and some elements of those countries adopted Christianity as their religion. However, from the tenth century onwards, Islam was the principal faith in many areas, especially areas closer to the Sahara, over which great desert Islam came from the Arab peoples who took over the Mediterranean lands of Africa, from Egypt to Morocco in the seventh century. The Arabic language accompanied the Islamic faith, and over the past millenium many West African Muslims have written works in Arabic: theology, law, history, poetry, and official documents of all kinds. The Arabic script was also adopted by the speakers of some African languages, in order to be able to write their own languages, since they had no indigenous script to do so. Arabic, hence, became like "the Latin of Africa" ,[3] following how Latin had been used as a literary language in Europe in medieval times, and having its script adopted for writing European languages. In West Africa, Kanuri, spoken just north of Lake Chad, was one of the first to be written in the Arabic script, and then Fulfulde (the language of the Fulbe/ Fulani), and later on Hausa, Wolof, and Yoruba. In the colonial era, from the late nineteenth century to the mid-twentieth century, the French, or the British, promoted understanding of their own languages and writing of them in the Latin script, and this script was soon also used for writing African languages in colonial territories.

In the following section take a look at the huge river that interconnects many regions of West Africa.

does Bambara have a written component?

or do ty just speak words?

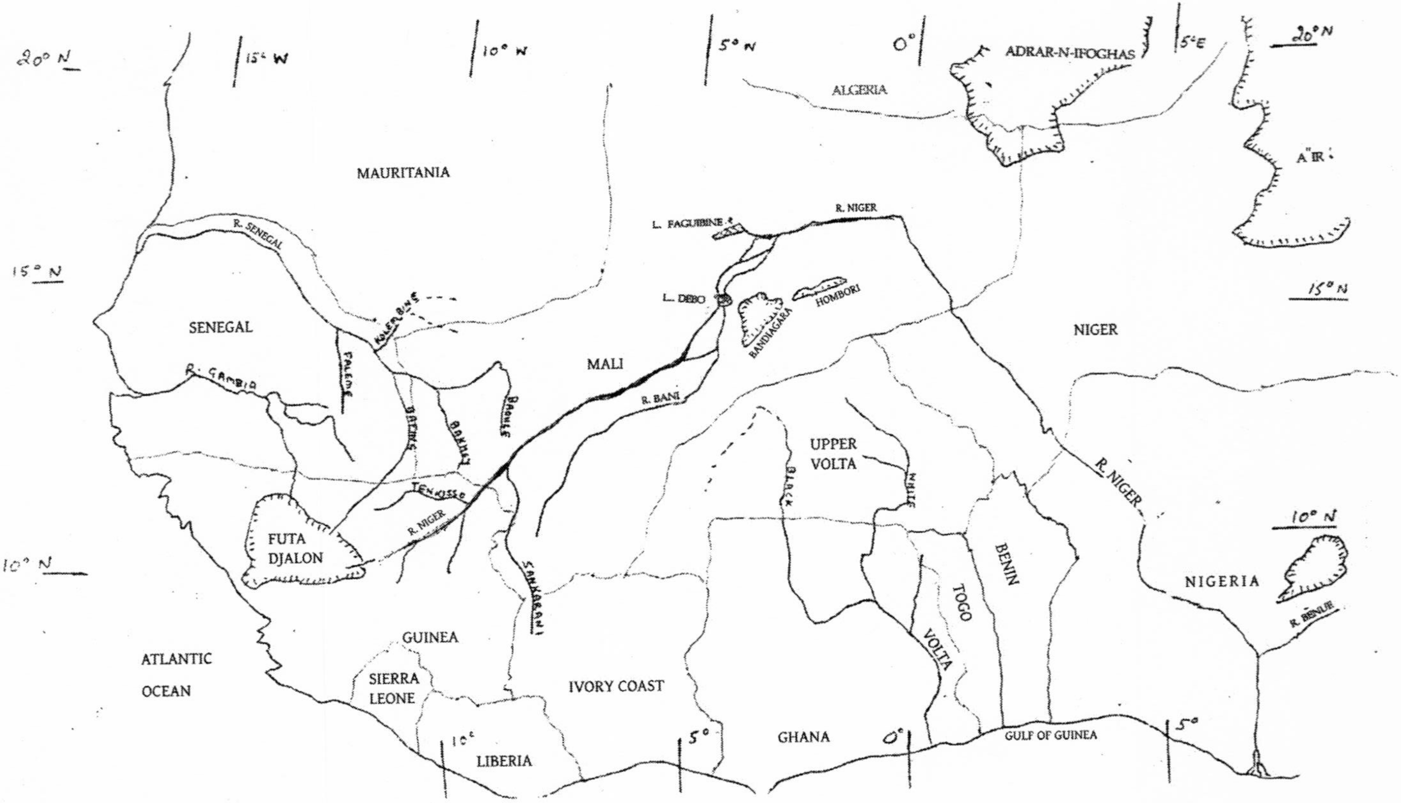

20° N
15° W
10° W
5° N
0°
5° E
20° N
ADRAR-N-IFOGHAS
ALGERIA
A"IR
MAURITANIA
R. SENEGAL
15° N
L. FAGUIBINE
R. NIGER
L. DEBO
BANDIAGARA
HOMBORI
15° N
SENEGAL
NIGER
R. GAMBIA
MALI
FALEME
R. BANI
BAFING
BAKHOY
BAOULE
UPPER VOLTA
BLACK
WHITE
TENKISSO
R. NIGER
FUTA DJALON
10° N
R. NIGER
10° N
BENIN
NIGERIA
TOGO
SANKARANI
R. BENUE
VOLTA
GUINEA
ATLANTIC OCEAN
SIERRA LEONE
IVORY COAST
10°
LIBERIA
5°
GHANA
0°
GULF OF GUINEA
5°

(ii) The River Niger[4]

At 2,585 miles in length, the river Niger is the third longest river in Africa, after the White Nile and the R. Zaïre, and the fourteenth longest in the world. It rises in the Kouranko mountains on the Sierra Leone-Guinée border at latitude 9° 5' N., less than two hundred miles from the Atlantic Ocean, and flows north and east into the southern Sahara at latitude 17° N., then finally south and east until it enters the Atlantic Ocean through a broad delta in Nigeria. Among the Mande people of Mali it is known as the Joliba, and among the Songhay of the great bend in the river it is called the Issa Ber, while, among the Nupe and Yoruba of Nigeria, it is called the Kwara.

Originally, Arab writers called it 'the 'Nile', assuming that the R. Niger and the R. Senegal were one, flowing into the Atlantic Ocean, and believing that all this was a westward branch of the true river Nile that flowed into the Mediterranean Sea. The geographer al-Idrīsī, wrote:

> In this [fourth] section [of the first Clime] occurs the splitting of the two Niles. I mean the Nile of Egypt which cuts through the land and flows from south to north. Most of the towns of Egypt are on both banks of it and on its islands also. The second part of the Nile flows from the east to the far west and on this part of the Nile are all the towns of the Blacks, or most of them. These two Niles have a common source in the Mountain of Q-m-r—the first part of which is sixteen degrees beyond the equator. The source of the Nile is in this mountain from ten springs. Five of these pour forth and gather in a large swamp; the other five also flow into another swamp. From each of these swamps three rivers flow, all of which empty into a single very large swamp.

The name 'Niger' is of uncertain origin, but first appears in European literature in *Della discrittione dell'Africa* ['Description of Africa'] of Leo Africanus in the mid-sixteenth century. It is possible that he took it from an Arabic translation of the 'Geography' of the Graeco-Egyptian scholar Claudius Ptolemaeus (*fl.* 150 A.D.), and that it is related to the Berber word 'gher' meaning 'river'. The Berber-speaking Oulimiden of Niger call the river 'Gher n'Igheren'—'river of rivers'.

The river has a number of notable natural features. After descending from the highlands of Guinée it becomes a broad slow-moving mass of water, about 1,000 yards wide at Bamako, the capital of Mali, and is joined by other smaller rivers, notably the R. Sankarani, upstream from Bamako, and the R. Bani, which flows into it in the southern reaches of the next notable feature, the Inland Delta. When the R. Niger enters this flat plain just beyond Segu it bifurcates into a number of subsidiary channels, creating a network of waterways that overflow their banks when the run-off of the heavy annual rains (over 80 in. a year), that fall in the highlands of Sierra Leone and Guinée, brings down flood waters in late August. Over the coming months this flood creates a massive shallow lake-type area up to 150 miles wide and 300 miles in length,[5] while at the northern end of this flood zone are a number of lakes, of more or less permanent nature, that are replenished by the annual flood. Like the R. Nile in Egypt, this annual flood lays down a rich layer of silt that makes the region an ideal agricultural zone, where grains can be grown for human consumption, and various grasses, clover, and similar plants, for horses and cattle to graze on.

The flood zone reaches as far north as Kabara, the port of Timbuktu, and in good years a channel used to reach Timbuktu some seven miles away from the river bed, though blocked up since *c.*1980. In former times this rendered the city an ideal meeting place for caravan traffic and riverine transportation, whilst its proximity to the larger flood zone assured its supply of grain. Prior to about 7,500 B.C. the Niger flowed northwards of Timbuktu and terminated in an inland delta in the Azawad region. During this wet period another independent river rose in the Adrar-n-Ifogha highlands, some 250 miles east, and flowed south to the Atlantic. At some stage this more easterly river 'captured' the western river, forming the present course of the R. Niger. Eventually, as the Sahara began to desiccate after 5000 B.C, the eastern river dried up, though flood torrents still course down stretches of valleys leading to the Niger during brief and erratic annual rains in July-August. Downstream from Kabara the Niger becomes narrower again, passing through the gorge of Tossay before turning south on its journey towards the sea. Just north of the Mali-Niger border the river passes over a series of shallow rapids (cataracts), which, before the construction of the Markala dam near Sansanding, were the only impediment to navigation before reaching the rapids of Kolikoro near Bamako where another dam now stands. This long stretch of navigable river made the R. Niger a very important waterway for the transportation of foodstuffs, trade goods, and persons, even for fighting men during the period of the Songhay empire (*c.* 1468–1591).

There are more notable rapids at Boussa in Nigeria where the Scottish traveler Mungo Park lost his life in 1806, but from thereon there is an unimpeded flow down to the delta. Mid-nineteenth century European explorers and traders could bring sea-going vessels up as far as Rabah (a little over 100 miles downstream from Boussa), though in the low-water season they sometimes ran aground on sand bars. Some 250 miles from the Atlantic, the river Niger is joined by another major watercourse, the river Benue which brings down water from the hills of Adamawa, an area straddling Nigeria and Cameroun. Together they flow due south to the sea, their silt building up a broad fan-shaped delta dissected by numerous channels creating swampland, in which mangroves flourish.

Many diverse peoples live along the banks of the Niger. Of these the largest groups are the Bamana (or Bambara) in the region between Bamako and Segu, the Songhay around the northern and eastern reaches of the great bend in the river, merging into the related Jerma (or Zarma) in Niger; and the Nupe in central Nigeria, the Igbo along the southern reaches of the river, and the Ijo (or Ijaw) living in the delta area. We should also mention the Sorko, Songhay-speaking fisherfolk, hippopotamus hunters, and boatbuilders, who move up and down the Niger from the Gulbin Kebbi tributary in Nigeria round to the Inland Delta, where groups with similar functions, the Bozo and Somonou, are to be found.

At the present time the river is not seriously polluted, since little major industry is sited along its banks. There are now several bridges across it: two in Bamako, one at Segu, one at Niamey the capital of Niger, one at Malanville on the borders of the states of Bénin and Niger, and several in Nigeria: one just south of the Kainji dam, two at Jebba (road and rail), one at Koton-Karifi (just upstream from the Niger-Benue confluence), one at Ajaokuta (where an iron and steel complex is sited) and one at Asaba-Onitsha linking the south-eastern and south-western quarters of Nigeria. A ferry links Gao in north-eastern Mali to a road that runs back to the capital, Bamako, and now there is a ferry from Kabara to the right bank of the Niger to join to a track leading to the road from Gao to Bamako. There is a major high dam at Kainji in Nigeria completed in the late 1960s and creating a lake that flooded old Boussa. Its hydro-electric turbines are a major source of electricity for Nigeria and Bénin.

The full course of the R. Niger was not drawn on European maps until after 1830. Hitherto European dependence on medieval Arab maps had led map-makers to posit a connection between the R. Niger and the R. Nile or to show the Niger originating in a lake (in the general region of Lake Chad) and flowing westwards to Senegal. The theory favored by Arabic geographers, such as al-Idrīsī (who wrote his *Nuzhat al-mushtaq* for the Norman king Roger II of Sicily in 1150), was that of a single river source in central Africa which flowed via two lakes and various branches into a vast swamp (roughly in what is now southern Sudan). Out of this swamp flowed the two 'Niles', one going north to Egypt and the other flowing west—the *Nīl al-sūdān*, 'Nile of the Blacks'—and emptying into the Atlantic Ocean in Senegal. Al-Idrīsī's work was published in Rome in 1592 and an Italian translation followed in 1600. Leo Africanus's 'Description', published in Italian in 1550, also appeared to confirm an east-west flow. The real west-east flow of the river was finally established by Mungo Park, when he saw the river near Segu in 1799, and he traced its course during his second journey as far as Boussa. Still searching for its outlet to the sea, Capt. Hugh Clapperton was told by Sultan Muḥammad Bello of Sokoto (Nigeria) in 1824 that the 'Nile/Niger' flowed on towards Egypt. Other authorities proposed that it drained into a swamp in the L. Chad region, or flowed on to join the R. Congo [Zaire]. In 1830 Clapperton's servant, Richard Lander, with his brother John, undertook an expedition that finally established the course of the river below Boussa, and showed that it flowed into the Atlantic Ocean through its delta in the Bight of Benin.

The lower reaches of the Niger soon became a 'highway' for European–more particularly British—explorers, missionaries, and merchants. The Lander brothers were recruited by MacGregor Laird for an exploratory trading mission in 1832, in which 39 out of 48 Europeans fell prey to disease. In 1849 two naval captains, William Allen and Bird Allen, together with D. H. Trotter, set off on a new expedition to supress slavery, open up legitimate trade, and establish a small settlement on the banks of the R. Niger. Missionaries, including (later Bishop) Samuel Crowther, a freed Yoruba slave from Sierra Leone, accompanied them. Again, the toll from malaria and other tropical diseases was heavy, and nothing permanent resulted. More successful was the Scottish doctor William Baikie, who commanded an expedition up the Niger in 1852, and on a second expedition in 1857, pushed up into Nupe country, signing a treaty with its emir, and creating a more permanent settlement at Lokoja on the Niger-Benue confluence. These expeditions paved the way for the activities of the Royal Niger company, founded in 1886, which, under its chief officer George Taubman Golgie, not only gained a commercial monopoly on the lower Niger region, but also political and military influence along the Niger. It thus became the precursor of more formal British colonial control. In 1898, Brigadier-General Frederick Lugard was dispatched to the area to halt French attempts to push into the Niger valley through their colony of Dahomey (Bénin), and his efforts ended with the conquest of most of what became [British] Northern Nigeria by 1903.[6]

Elsewhere on the Niger, far upstream from what is now Mali, the French began to move in from their colony of Senegal in the 1880s, dismantling, piece by piece, the Islamic empire established by *al-ğājj* ʿUmar al-Fūtī (d. 1864), based on Segu and, after his death, divided among his sons. In 1892 Col. Archinard took Segu, and seized its royal library that was sent back to France, and it still kept at the Bibliothèque in Paris.[7] By 1894 French forces had conquered territory as far inland as Timbuktu, and by the end of the nineteenth century they had completed the conquest of the territories bordering the R. Niger right around to the area thatr the British were busily bringing under their control in what became 'Nigeria'. By 1960, however, both the British and the French had withdrawn from their colonial territories along the Niger, and four independent nations had emerged: Guinée, Mali, Niger and Nigeria.

Within Mali the river Niger remains a path of transportation–even sometimes used by tourists–with ferries moving from Kolikoro, near Bamako, to Mopti, and to Kabara (the 'port' of Timbuktu), and to Gao. The period of the year in which these various sectors of the river are run through by ferries, depends on the season of flooding that provides deep enough water for sailing.

Chapter Two

Northern Africa's Links with Sub-Saharan Africa

This essay deals mainly with contacts between northern Africa and West Africa in the Islamic period, i.e. after the seventh century A.D. However, here are a few preliminary words on the period preceding this.

The Period before the Rise of Islam

The area we now call the Sahara (from an Arabic word [*ṣaḥrā'*] meaning 'desert') has appeared and disappeared several times during the history of human kind. Most recently it began to emerge during a period of continuing dessication, beginning from about 2,500 B.C. By around 300 B.C. the process was almost complete and the herding populations that had once inhabited the grasslands of the Sahara had dispersed north and south.[1] Isolated groups of agriculturalists remained behind in better watered areas, and their descendants form the basal element of the darker-skinned low status agriculturalists, known as the nomads who are to be found in oases from southern Morocco to the Niger river. The oases of the Fezzan in southern Libya probably also originally contained similar populations; an early Islamic legal text describes the Fezzanis as 'one of the peoples of the blacks'. As the Sahara dried up, contact between the populations of the Mediterranean African lands and those of West Africa gradually diminished, but not before knowledge of copper and iron working had passed into West Africa around the middle of the first millenium B.C.. Early in the Christian era the introduction, from the Middle East, of the one-humped camel (*Camelus dromedarius*) made a nomadic existence in the Sahara possible, and Berber-speaking groups began to move deeper into the desert. Those who have come to be known as the Tuareg appear to have originated in Libya, perhaps obtaining camels from Roman legions stationed there, and then moved south and west, eventually occupying large areas of modern Niger, southern Algeria and northern Mali. In the West the Sanhaja, like the Tuareg wearers of the face-veil (*lithām*), moved into the deserts lying between the southern Atlas, the R. Senegal and the R. Niger.

Both of these nomadic groups played an important role in sustaining contact between Mediterranean and sub-Saharan Africa, especially during the Islamic period, when their intimate knowledge of the Sahara and their camel resources made possible the organization and safe passage of trading caravans. Prior to the Islamic era there was very little direct commerce between the two sides of the Sahara. Rock drawings of horse-drawn chariots (probably belonging to the first millenium B.C.) point to possible routes from Fezzan to the Niger around Gao and from western Algeria through western Mauritania and then eastwards to the Niger at the northern end of the Inland Delta. However, their significance is difficult to gauge, and it is unlikely that such fragile vehicles and sensitive animals could have served the needs of either regular commerce or periodic warfare. A trans-Saharan trade in gold in late Roman times has been argued for, but the evidence is tenuous. Romans had other more accessible sources of gold, and on the West African side there is little evidence of the emergence of significant polities until after the middle of the first millenium A.D. Certainly, North Africans had contacts with Saharan oases and there were various Roman exploratory probes into the Sahara and warfare with the Garamantes of the Fezzan; but fuller, more direct and substantial contacts between North Africa and sub-Saharan Africa only become apparent after the establishment in the seventh/eighth centuries A.D. of a huge Islamic empire that stretched from the Atlantic in the west to the Indus in the east.

The Islamic Period (c. 670–1900)

The Arab conquest of North Africa began in earnest with the founding of the garrison city of Qayrawān (Cairouan in modern Tunisia) in 670 A.D. By the early years of the eighth century a strip of territory 100–200 miles deep had been brought under Arab control all the way from the borders of Egypt to the Atlantic coast, with significant southerly extensions into the Fezzan and into the Sus region of southern Morocco. From both of these regions, probes were undertaken into lands to the south, but no conquests took place. Early trading contacts probably began in the latter part of the eighth century following the arrival of schismatic Khārijites of the Ibāḍī and Ṣufī sects who sought refuge in North Africa from determined attempts by the ʿAbbāsid caliphs (from 750 A.D.) to stamp them out in the central lands of Islam. These sectarians established themselves in areas relatively remote from the Arab garrisons: in Jabal Nafūsa (a mountainous region south of Tripoli), in Tozeur in the marshy Jarīd region of southern Ifrīqiya(Tunisa), in Tahart in the central Atlas Mountains (Algeria) and at Sijilmasa, an oasis in Tafilalt beyond the Moroccan Atlas. From these locations they established trading contacts with existing or emerging polities on the Saharan fringes of West Africa.

The principal trade routes of the early centuries of Islam appear to have been the following: a westerly route from Sijilmasa down to Awdaghast (Tegdaoust in S. Mauritania), and from there to the kingdom of Ancient Ghana astride the region between the R. Senegal and the R. Niger; an easterly route from Jabal Nafūsa through the Fezzan and down through the Kawār oasis towards the Lake Chad region where the kingdom of Kanem emerged in the late tenth century; and a central route from Tahart via Warghla (where it was joined by a route from Tozeur) down to the Niger at Kawkaw (i.e. Gawgaw or Gao). These routes were apparently established by the early ninth century, since the names Ghana, Kawkaw, and Zaghāwa (a nomadic group associated with the founding of the Kanem kingdom) appear in the *Ṣūrat al-arḍ* of al-Khwārizmī, an early work of geography, otherwise mainly based on the *Geographia* of Claudius Ptolemaius (*c.* 150 A.D.), and written between 813 and 842 A.D.

These three axes remained the principal avenues of trade between Mediterranean and Sudanic Africa down to the early twentieth century, though precise routes varied from period to period. From early on, there was also a transverse route which connected Ancient Ghana with Egypt via the Middle Niger, the Aïr massif and Fezzan, and various sectors of it remained active over the centuries, especially as a route for pilgrims making for Mecca. By about the mid-fifteenth century, the northern Hausa cities of Kano and Katsina (Nigeria) were linked more directly to trans-Saharan trade by routes that led north through Agades, or the Tegidda region to the west of it to Ghadames and Tripoli, or north-west to Touat and thence to Tlemcen and Fez. In the seventeenth century, after the conversion of the ruler of Wadai (in eastern Chad) to Islam, a route was opened up from the Lake Chad region to Dar Fur and the Nile valley, leading to Mecca via the Red Sea, and to Egypt down the Nile valley. A route also led up from Wadai through the Kufra oasis to Benghazi. This latter route was especially active after Sanusi *zāwiyas* were established in southern Chad in the late nineteenth century, and was probably the last route used for bringing slaves across the Sahara.

The items traded across the Sahara in both directions were many and varied. Southward went horses, rock salt, cloths, both of European (from the fifteenth century at any rate) and North African weave (especially the thick blanket material called *hanbal* corrupted to *lambens* by the Portuguese), swords, chain mail, and horse trappings, copper and brass vessels (brass bowls from Mamlūk Egypt have turned up in modern Ghana, having been used as local shrine objects), mirrors, scissors, needles, perfumes, paper, and cowrie shells (*Cypraea moneta*, brought from the Indian Ocean), which were used as currency in several states bordering the Sahara.[2] Northwards went slaves, ivory (and perhaps hippopotamus tusks), grain (to Saharan oases) goat hides, senna, and cola nuts (*Cola nitida*), amongst other items of tropical produce. There is little doubt, however, that it was the lure of gold that was the primary incentive for North African merchants to undertake the perils of a Saharan crossing. Al-Fāzārī, an astronomer contemporary with al-Khwarazmī, characterized [ancient] Ghana as 'the land of gold' and gold is the *Leitmotif* of all subsequent Arab writing about the region. Gold dust was obtained from pits in Bambuhu, a region lying between the Faleme and Bafing, southern tributaries of the R. Senegal, and somewhat later from Bure on tributaries of the upper Niger. From the late fourteenth century Muslim traders also obtained gold mined in the Akan forests (in modern Ghana) bringing it up to Jenne and thence to Walata or Timbuktu. The most important item bartered for the gold was rock salt, obtained from pits in the central Sahara (Idjil, Taghaza, Taodeni and others less easily identified), carried down to the R. Niger or R. Senegal on the backs of camels and loaded onto large river canoes. As late as the 1970s this trade was still in existence, though no gold was then being exchanged for the salt.

Far to the east in Kanem there was no gold to trade in, and the chief commodity was most probably slaves. Earlier the Romans had obtained slaves via intermediaries from the Tibesti massif to the north of Kanem, so a southerly extension of this trade should not surprise us. Black slaves appear in the North African record as early as 826, as laborers engaged in a revolt in the Jarid area, and later in that century the Aghlabids of Ifriqiya used some as soldiers. In fact, slaves became the second major item of commerce in the trans-Saharan trade along all routes, right down to the early years of the twentieth century. Prior to the nineteenth century, slaves were most often bartered for Barbarye horses, in ratios of up to fifteen slaves for one horse, depending on time and place, and the age and sex of the slaves. Although horses were to be found in West Africa before the Islamic era, they were small compared to the Barbary horse which could carry a rider wearing chain or quilted mail, thus furnishing a war machine or a long distance raider—both usages serving to provide yet more slaves for exchange. The slaves thus transported to North Africa were primarily used in domestic service including concubinage (two-thirds of the slaves taken over the Sahara in the nineteenth century were females). The next most common usage was as soldiers. Many regimes thus employed them, while in Morocco under *Mūlāy* Ismāʿīl (1672–1727) a vast slave army was raised by impounding all black slaves and ex-slaves in the Moroccan lands, the army's strength being later maintained by marrying the male slaves to black female slaves and training up the resultant offspring—boys for the army, and girls for palace service. Relatively few slaves were used for agricultural or industrial tasks, the opportunity in North Africa for intensive labor in such occupations being restricted. Some were re-exported. Prior to 1492 some black slaves were sold into Andalusia. From the seventeenth century the trans-Saharan slave trade provided the Ottoman sultans with eunuchs to guard the harem of the Topkapi palace,[3] while others were sent to serve in the Prophet's mosque in Medina or the Mosque of the Kaʿba in Mecca.

In the absence of an Arab-Muslim conquest of West Africa, the way was open for political relations between Sudanic and Mediterranean African states, based on mutual interest. The way was also open for the conversion of West Africans to Islam at their own pleasure, devoid of the pressures brought by conquest and colonization. In the eleventh century—some two and a half centuries after initial contacts—a number of rulers of states on the southern Saharan fringes formally accepted Islam: e.g. the ruler of Takrūr, a small state on the R. Senegal, the ruler of the state based on Gao (Kawkaw), perhaps as early as the late tenth century, and the ruler of the state of Kanem. It was in the same century that a militant religious movement arose in the western Sahara among the nomads of the Sanhaja. These Almoravids, as they became known (from Arabic *al-murābiṭūn*—'warriors for the faith') attacked Sijilmasa *c.* 1055, swept on into central Morocco, and before the end of the century into Andalusia, briefly uniting a vast region from central Spain to the southern Sahara under their banner. Their role in the demise of Ancient Ghana is disputed, as is the possible role of a segment of the movement in the affairs of the state based on Gao. Tombstones recording the deaths of 'kings' and 'queens' buried there in the period 1088–1120 have been shown to originate in Almeria, then under Almoravid control, but the precise identity of these royals is unclear.

Sudanic [sub-Saharan] states established diplomatic relations with North African and Middle Eastern states at various times. Kanem exchanged gifts with the Ḥafṣids of Tunis in the thirteenth century; Mali had close ties with the Marīnids of Fez in the mid-fourteenth century; Bornu's rulers turned to the Mamlūk sultan of Egypt for help against marauding Arab nomads later in the same century, and, in the late sixteenth century, sent missions to the Ottoman sultan Murād III and to the Saʿdian sultan of Morocco Aḥmad al-Manṣūr in a bid to obtain firearms. Subsequent rulers of Bornu maintained close relations with the Ottoman governors of Tripoli, during the seventeenth century. Relations between Songhay under the *askiyas* (rulers, 1493–1591) and the Saʿdians were less friendly. The Saʿdians used both diplomacy and force to wrest the salt pans of Taghāza from Songhay's control, and in 1591 a Saʿdian force dominated by Spanish renegades crossed the Sahara and overthrew the reigning *askiya* of Songhay, Isḥāq II. From then on, until the early nineteenth century, the Middle Niger was governed by descendants of these and other Moroccan soldiery sent to Timbuktu, who ruled with the title *bāshā* [Pasha]. Even in the late nineteenth century the citizens of Timbuktu appealed to the ʿAlawid sultan of Morocco to protect them against the invading French—needless to say, with no avail.

Religious and Cultural Relations

Whatever the military impact of the Almoravid movement on the region may have been, one thing seems sure. It was in the wake of this movement that the Mālik school (*madh'hab*) of Islamic law—the school vigorously promoted by the Almoravids—became dominant in West Africa. Until today, its sway is undisputed, even though in the twentieth century its scope was mainly limited to family law.[4] The principal law books of the school, still studied with their manifold commentaries until today, originate from North Africa, where the school also predominates, and Egypt. West African scholars themselves have written many a commentary or gloss on the *Risāla* of Ibn Abī Zayd of Qayrawān (d. 997) and the *Mukhtaṣar* of Khalīl b. Isḥāq of Alexandria (d. 1374), as they have also studied, taught, and commented, upon the writings of many another Muslim scholar of North Africa, Andalusia, and Egypt.

Historically, relatively few West African scholars went to North Africa to study, though many visited Egypt on their way to, or from, their pilgrimage to Mecca. North African scholars, however, did visit West Africa, sometimes spending years teaching or holding judicial positions. Among the most influential was Muḥammad b. ʿAbd al-Karīm al-Maghīlī (d. 1504) from Tlemcen, who spent some years in both Kano and Gao and advised their rulers in the 1490s. He is said to have left behind some male children in Kano, and their putative descendants still play a role in Kano court and religious life. Since the nineteenth century, a religious movement, originating in Morocco, has had a profound influence in West Africa. The Tijānī 'congregation', a Ṣufi 'way' (*ṭarīqa*) owes its origins to the teachings of Sīdī Aḥmad al-Tijānī (d. 1815), a mystic from ʿAin Māḍī in the Algerian Sahara. Disciples of his spread his teachings in Mauritania and from there the 'Way' was carried into what are now Senegal and Guinée. *Al-Ḥājj* ʿUmar b. Saʿīd (d. 1864), a scholar from Futa Toro (Senegal) was made a secondary leader of the Tijānī 'Way', by a deputy of al-Tijānī, during his pilgrimage to Mecca. On his return to West Africa he recruited disciples and eventually led a militant movment (*jihād*), which carved out a considerable state in what is now Mali. On his way home, he had initiated a number of people into the 'Way' in Bornu and Sokoto (Nigeria). In the 1930s–1960s the Tijānī 'Way' garnered large numbers of adherents in Senegal, in Ghana, and in northern Nigeria, through the exertions of Shaykh Ibrahim Niasse (d. 1975) of Kaolak (Senegal), who gained international repute within the order, and within such pan-Islamic organizations as the World Islamic League.

North African culture has influenced West Africa in many domains other than the purely religious. Domestic and royal architecture along the Saharan fringes show signs of such influence, especially in the flat-roofed, cube-shaped houses, and the multiple courtyards of palaces with distinct 'harem' quarters. Styles of men's robes also show North African influence, and the narrow men's loom was probably introduced from there, though having more distant origins. Some food crops came to West Africa from the Mediterranean lands, especially through returning pilgrims. Onions and tomatoes are two of the more important of such items, while names for maize often reveal its path of introduction: *masar hayni* in Songhay and *dawar masara* in Hausa both mean 'Egyptian millet', while the Tamacheq word for maize '*makka*' clearly hints at the pilgrimage route. Above all, there has been a strong influence of the Arabic language and script in the cultural life of sub-Saharan African Muslims. Arabic was the principal language of literacy for a thousand years down to the colonial period, and the forms of Arabic script used in West Africa all derive from North African or Andalusian hands. Many African languages have been written using slightly modified forms of the Arabic script (e.g. Fulfulde, Hausa, Kanuri, Wolof),[5] though this has now been largely abandoned in favor of the Roman script. West African languages spoken by Muslim peoples have absorbed a considerable number of Arabic loan words, some of them through North African dialectal usage.

There have also been influences the other way. Some of the Arabic writings of West African Muslim scholars such as Aḥmad Bābā of Timbuktu (d. 1627), Muḥammad b. Muḥammad of Katsina (d. 1742), Ṣāliḥ al-Fullānī of Futa Jallon (d. 1804), and Muḥammad Bello of Sokoto (d. 1837) found their way into North Africa and the Middle East; Ṣāliḥ al-Fullānī, who had a noted teaching career in Medina (Saudi Arabia), became better known in India than in West Africa.[6] Bornu was famous for its Qur'anic calligraphy and copies of the sacred text penned there were sold for high prices in Tripoli. At another level, the *bori* possession cult practiced among the Hausa (more particularly by non-Muslims) was carried into Tunis and Tripoli by slaves, while the so-called *dīwāns* of Sīdī Bilāl, quasi-islamized possession and exorcism cults, that have flourished in Algeria (as well as other sacrificial cults), have West African origins; as does the *gnawa* cult (*cf.* Berber *igginaw*—'black') long practised in Morocco, but now reduced to the status of 'folklore' and 'performed' for tourists.

Finally, we may recall that the writings of medieval Arab authors from North Africa, Andalusia, and Egypt, constitute the sole written sources for the history of West Africa before the arrival of Europeans on the coast in the fifteenth century and the beginnings of local historiographical traditions in Arabic in the sixteenth.[7] Such sources have many weaknesses, of course: notably the lack of first-hand knowledge of West Africa on the part of most of their authors, continued dependence on ancient Greek writers (notably Claudius Ptolemaius of Alexandria, *fl.* 150 A.D.), and certain prejudiced notions about black people, partly derived from such sources, and partly from the close relationship of blackness to slavery in the Arab world. Three authors, however, benefited extensively from information gathered from visitors to the region, or from West Africans who visited the Arab world: al-Bakrī (d. 1087), an Andalusian, who has left us a precious description of Ancient Ghana; al-ʿUmarī (d. 1349), a Syrian who wrote an encyclopedia for bureaucrats, which included a description of Ancient Mali; and Ibn Khaldūn (d. 1406), who gave a brief dynastic history of Mali in his general history of Islamic civilization. To these we should add the account of the great fourteenth-century world traveler Ibn Baṭṭūṭa, who visted Mali and the Middle Niger region in 1352–3 and described these regions from the point of view of a tourist.[8]

The Contemporary Period

Physical links between North and West Africa have become tenuous with the cessation of caravan traffic. The French dreamed of building a trans-Saharan railway to link their territory in Algeria with their West African possessions via Timbuktu, but this was never more than a dream. Although there is now a paved road from Algiers to the central Algerian Sahara at Adrar in Tuwāt, and a similar one from Cotonou in the Republic of Bénin to the Niger-Mali border, this still leaves a gap of some 900 miles. As of 1994, traffic on land routes through Mali and Niger was virtually at a halt, since militant action by Tuareg nomads, seeking greater autonomy, had rendered the area insecure. Air services between the two regions of Africa are few and far between, and travel between West and North Africa is often taken via Paris or Rome. North African states retain diplomatic representation in the more West African important capitals such as Abuja (Nigeria), Accra (Ghana), Abidjan (Ivory Coast) and Dakar (Senegal), and this is reciprocated by those countries in Rabat, Algiers, Tunis and Tripoli. However, all the countries of both regions belonged to the Organization of African Unity [now the African Union] and many also belong to the Organization of the Islamic Conference, the cultural Division of which is based in Rabat and is active in West African countries.

Part II

Islam

Chapter Three

Islam in West Africa

After the death of the Prophet Muhammad in 632 A.D., Arab Muslim forces overtook most elements of the Byzantine-ruled areas of the Middle East, and then in moved into the African continent, taking over Egypt from the Byzantines, and then moving westwards along North Africa. They reached what is now Tunisia and established their fortress-town at Qayrawān in 670, and by the end of the seventh century they had occupied land up to the coast of the Atlantic Ocean, though not taking over territory very far south of the Mediterranean Sea.

Importantly for them, the Berber populations of their occupied territories mostly converted to Islam. In this way Islam passed on to Saharan nomads, particularly the Berber Sanhaja of the western Sahara. With a renewal and growth of their faith in the mid-eleventh century, the Sanhaja formed a movement, known as the Almoravids (*al-Murābiṭūn*), that then occupied all of the region of modern Morocco, and moved into the area of Spain formally overtaken by Arab Muslims. As widespread Saharan nomads, their faith to Islam soon began to have influence on West African "black" populations. The Massufa clan of the Sanhaja migrated along the southern region of the Sahara in the late eleventh century, some of them settling in Walata, Sane (near Gao) and the Takedda region; some Sanhaja took up an area that later became Timbuktu, and, indeed, it was some Sanhaja scholars who later made Timbuktu a major center of Islamic learning.

Among early West Africans to adopt Islam were the Dyula (also called Wangara), a clan of the Mande ethnic group, the rest of which later became Muslims. The Dyula mainly engaged in trade and moved widely around West

Africa, influencing other peoples to adopt Islam. Another important ethnic group to largely adopt Islam was the Fulani (also known as the Fulbe or Fulfulde), nomadic cattle owners, who moved from the edge of the southern Sahara down into the Inland Delta of the Nile river, and then elements of them moved to other areas, such as Futa Toro and Futa Jallon, and eventually moved eastwards, into northern Nigeria, and on to Chad and Dār Fūr. By the ninth century, North African Muslims (Arab/Berber) began to cross the Sahara for trade, including to obtain slaves; and no doubt they had influence of conversion on the rulers they contacted.

Among the early and most celebrated persons converted to Islam were a number of rulers in the Sahel zone: the ruler of Takrūr, in the Senegal river area; the king of the Zuwa dynasty in Gao, and the ruler of Kanem, just north of Lake Chad. All of these conversions were in the eleventh century. Later, rulers of major empires promoted Islam, making pilgrimages to Mecca; e.g. Mansā Mūsā of Mali in 1324, and Askiya *al-ḥājj* Muḥammad of the Songhay Empire in 1497.[1] As a pious Muslim, Askiya *al-ḥājj* Muḥammad gave support to the Islamic community of Timbuktu, a city of Muslims ever since its initiation in the early twelfth century. Muslim scholars migrated there from North Africa and from Saharan oases, and when Mansā Mūsā returned from his pilgrimage, he stopped in Timbuktu in 1325 and had built the "Great Mosque" (*Jingere Ber*), a Muslim shrine soon afterwards to be added to with the large Sankore mosque. The most celebrated scholarly clan to settle in Timbuktu was the Aqīt family of the Sanhaja Massufa, coming to Timbuktu *c.* 1450 from Māsina in the south of the Inland Delta.

Many works on aspects of Islam—especially on *sharīʿa*—were written in Arabic in Timbuktu, especially in the fifteenth to seventeenth centuries, and even down to the twentieth scentury. Some Muslim scholars possessed large libraries of such manuscripts—many still in existence—and in 1973 a huge public library of manuscripts was founded: the Ahmad Baba Center (Centre de Documentation et de Recherches Historiques Ahmad Baba [CEDRAB]). Aḥmad Bābā (1556–1627), after whom it was named, was one of the most celebrated Timbuktu scholars, a member of the Aqīt family, though he was exiled to Morocco in 1594, returning home in 1608. He wrote nearly seventy works, and became celebrated in Morocco as well as in West Africa.

A West African scholar who once quoted him was the Fulani Usman ɗan Fodio (in Arabic: ʿUthmān b. Muḥammad Fūdī),[2] who set up a jihad in the Sokoto region of NW Nigeria in 1804, creating an Islamic empire out of most of the Hausa states of what is now northern Nigeria. His ancestors had migrated to that region from Futa Toro in the sixteenth century, though Islam had other influences in Hausaland. Kanem became an early Islamic state, and in the thirteenth century took over what is now Bornu, and from there, to the west of Lake Chad, Islam then had influence to farther west. There was also influence in one area of Hausaland from the Dyula. Some of them had moved south from Jenne to obtain gold being mined in what is now southern Ghana, to be taken to Jenne and then Timbuktu for trans-Saharan trade. When Songhay took over the Inland Delta in the 1470s, the Dyula decided to take the gold to a different trans-Saharan trading location, and so some of them went off to Kano, others of them having already converted the ruler of that city and state, a trading zone with trans-Saharan inter-connections.

Islam later became spread farther south in West Africa. In the second half of the seventeenth century some scholars moved from Timbuktu to the north of what is now the Republic of Ghana. In the same period some Dyula also settled in that area, and a century or more later Hausa migrants moved into the region, so the area between the Black and White Volta rivers became a new region of Islam, and by the nineteenth century a source of Arabic-Islamic writings. Similarly, in what is now Nigeria, Islam's influence moved south, following the early nineteenth century jihad that created the Sokoto Caliphate. The Nupe adopted Islam, and in 1824 the Yoruba town of Ilorin became part of the Caliphate, and soon produced Muslim scholars who wrote Arabic treatises. Some later moved south as far as Abeokuta and Lagos; notably Ādam al-Ilūrī (1917–1992), who set up at Agege, near Lagos, an Arabic and Islamic Training Centre in the mid-twentieth century, and published there many of his seventy Islamic writings and those of some of his colleagues.

West Africa became a major area of Islamic writings, mainly in Arabic, though some scholars used the Arabic script to write their own African languages. The major city of Arabic writing in the sixteenth and seventeenth centuries was Timbuktu, where several scholars had their own Arabic manuscript libraries. Although they might have in them local writings, some of them also obtained Arabic writings brought over the Sahara by North African traders, or copied items themselves while in Egypt, spending time there after making their pilgrimage to Mecca.

In the nineteenth century northern Nigeria became a powerful area of Islam, resulting from the jihad set up by the Fulani scholar Usmanu ɗan

Fodio [in Arabic: ʿUthmān b. Muḥammad Fūdī], who had the areas of Kano, Katsina and Zaria conquered, and he founded the city of Sokoto as the capital of what became the Sokoto Caliphate. He was a Fulani in origin, whose clan—the Fodiawa—came into that region from Futa Toro in the fifteenth century; and he and his brother ʿAbdullāh, and his son Muḥammad Bello, were abundant writers of Arabic works, with some items—notably poems—in Fulani.[3] Usmanu ɗan Fodio's daughter Asmāʾ also wrote poems in Fulani, and some in Arabic and some in Hausa.[4] As Islam spread into the southwestern area of Nigeria, Muslim scholars began Arabic writing in Ilorin, Lagos, and elsewhere, in the twentieth century, some even writing poems in the Yoruba language in Arabic script.

Muslim writers—mainly using Arabic–also existed in others areas in West Africa, mainly in, or after, the eighteenth century: e.g. Senegal, Guinea, Ivory Coast, and Ghana.[5]

Initially converted rulers in the Sahel region were those contacted by Muslim merchants from North Africa, and they obtained items for trading with them, notably non-Muslims seized as slaves, both male and female. Hence elements of 'black Africa' (*bilād al-sūdān*) became elements of 'Arab' Africa. Some of them converted to Islam, which led to their being freed, though many then remained in 'Arab' Africa. In Morocco many 'black' Africans were put into a military force in the early eighteenth century, on the assumption that all were slaves.

As for Sufi orders (*ṭariqas*), two carried strong spiritual influence on western Africa. The first was the Qādiriyya, originating in Baghdad in the twelfth century under the teachings of ʿAbd al-Qādir al-Jīlanī, and later being adopted in North Africa and by Saharan tribes, such as the Kunta—an Arab-Berber tribe containing intellectuals, originally in the Touat oasis and then, from the seventeenth century, moving south, split in two, with a major group just north of Timbuktu and, in part of the first half of the nineteenth century, governing Timbuktu. The Qādiriyya was also adopted in northern Nigeria (notably by ʿUthmān ibn Muḥammad Fūdī) and in Senegal. Another *tariqa*—the Tijāniyya overtook it in the nineteenth century, though not among the Kunta. Aḥmad al-Tijānī (1737–1815), the founder of that Sufi order, was born in the Algerian oasis of ʿAyn Maḍi, and then moved to Fez in Morocco. His teachings were adopted by the Idaw ʿAlī tribe of southern Mauritania, and then promoted by *al-Ḥājj* ʿUmar ibn Saʿīd of Futa Toro in Senegal, who later conquered much of present-day Mali. The Tijānī *ṭarīqa* became appreciated in Senegal and, led by the *shaykh* Ibrāhīm

Two major Sufi orders: Qādiriyya
Tijaniyya

Niasse (1902–1975), it was adopted by many West Africans as he traveled into Mali, Ghana, and Nigeria, and it also passed on to Chad and the Sudan. In Senegal another *ṭarīqa* was later created—the Mouride order, inspired by Aḥmad Bamba (1855–1927), originally a Qādirī. In the second half of the twentieth century, however, Sufi *ṭarīqas*–especially the Tijāniyya–were opposed by Africans who had spent time in Arabia, and come under the influence of the Wahhābiyya movement, opposing Sufism.

Northern Nigeria also had historians who wrote in Arabic. ʿUthmān b. Muḥammad Fūdī (Usmanu ɗan Fodio) wrote about his own *jihād* efforts to take control over the Hausa peoples of Sokoto and other north-western regions: *Bayān wujūb al-hijra ʿala ʾl-ʿibād.*[6] His brother ʿAbd Allah in 1813 wrote *Tazyīn al-waraqāt bi-jamʿ baʿḍ mā lī min al-abyāt*, an account of that *jihād*, with poems of his related to it. Muḥammad Bello also wrote a history of that *jihād*, together with other information on neighboring regions; *Infāq al-Maysūr fī ṭaʾrīkh bilād al-Takrūr.*[7]

Segu focuses a significant portion of the story line in the city of Timbuktu, providing an historical account of an important center of Islam.

Chapter Four

Timbuktu: A Famous West African City of Islam and Arabic Writing

Timbuktu's existence began at the end of the fifth century of the *hijra* (the beginning of the twelfth century A.D.), as a settlement for some nomads of the southern Sahara. This was described by the historian ʿAbd al-Raḥmān al-Saʿdī as follows:

> Timbuktu was founded by the .Maghsharan Tuareg towards the end of the fifth century of the *hijra*. They would come there in summer to graze their herds on the banks of the river at the village of .Amadia; where they encamped.[1] Then in the rainy season they would return northward by stages to .Arawān, their farthest point in the upper lands, and encamp there. Thus did they choose the location of this virtuous, pure, undefiled, and proud city, blessed with divine favor, a healthy climate, and [commercial] activity. It is a city unsullied by the worship of idols, where none has prostrated save to God the Compassionate, a refuge of scholarly and righteous folk, a haunt of saints and ascetics, and a meeting place of caravans and boats.[2]

In fact the nomads who resided in that location were members of the Masūfa tribe, a branch of the group of tribes all known together as the Ṣanhāja—members of the Almoravid movement of the eleventh century, as stated by al-Saʿdī later in his book.[3] In the fifteenth century the most celebrated scholars of Timbuktu were from the Masūfa.

As for the settlement location of those nomads, known as Timbuktu, it was close to the river known as the Nile in medieval Arabic writings, and as the Niger beginning with the writing of Leo Africanus (al-Ḥasan b. Muḥammad al-Wazzān al-Zayyātī[4]). Between the river and the city is a watercourse which only contains water in the flood season at the beginning of each year. To the north of Timbuktu are Saharan lands that stretch over to Morocco after the Touat oasis. Because of its geographical location, Timbuktu became a center for trade between tropical Africa (*bilād al-sūdān*) and the lands of the Mediterranean. Commercial links also came to exist between Timbuktu and the Saharan oases. On account of this Timbuktu became an attractive city for some individuals from North Africa and the oases.

In the year 1325, when Timbuktu was under the rule of Mali, the sultan of Mali, Mansā Mūsā, came there during his return from pilgrimage, and ordered the construction of a "Great Mosque"[5] (until now still in existence in the south of the city) under the supervision of the Andalusian scholar Abū Isḥāq al-Sāḥilī, who had accompanied Mansā Mūsā on his return journey from Mecca. Then after some years a large mosque was built in the Sankore quarter in the north of the city, financed by a woman from the Aghlāl, a religious Tuareg tribe (of *Ineslemen*). The Sankore mosque became a place for teaching *tafsīr* (Qurʾānic exegesis) and other Islamic teachings. Sankore was a dwelling place for many scholars, especially those belonging to the Masūfa.

One of the most important of them was a family called the Aqīt. Their ancestor Muḥammad Aqīt migrated from Māsina to Timbuktu around 1450, and his grandson Abū 'l-Thanāʾ Maḥmūd became imam of the Sankore mosque, and afterwards became *qāḍī* of Timbuktu for fifty years, during which time he wrote a commentary on the *Mukhtaṣar* of Khalīl b. Isḥāq.[6] After his death in 1548 he was succeeded as *qāḍī* of Timbuktu by his son Muḥammad until he himself died in 1565. Among the most important scholars of the Aqīt family were Aḥmad b. *al-ḥājj* Aḥmad b. ʿUmar b. Muḥammad Aqīt (d. 1583), and his son Aḥmad Bābā.

Aḥmad Bābā composed a very important book with the title *Nayl al-ibtihāj bi-taṭrīz al-Dībāj*, which is a collection of biographies of scholars of the Mālikī *madh'hab*.[7] It contains a description of his father as follows:

> He was—may God have mercy upon him—a smart and understanding scholar, highly accomplished, knowledgeable and versatile —a specialist in *ḥadīth*, in jurisprudence, rhetoric and logic. In 956 he travelled to the east, made pilgrimage and visited Medina. There he met a number of people, including al-Nāṣir al-Laqānī, *al-Sharīf* Yūsuf al-Armiyūṭī, a pupil of al-Suyūṭī, Jamāl al-Dīn Ibn *al-Shaykh* Zakariyyā,'. *al-Shaykh* al-Tājūrī, and [*al-Shaykh*] al-Ujhūrī.[8]

Pilgrimage and meeting with scholars in the Middle East was the practice of many scholars of Timbuktu, some of whom bought or copied manuscripts in the Islamic sciences.

Aḥmad Bābā himself was celebrated and has been kept in mind until the present day. In 1973 in Timbuktu a center for conserving manuscripts of the Timbuktu tradition was created using his name: Centre de Documentation et de Recherches Historiques Ahmad Baba (CEDRAB). Ahmad Baba was born in 1556 and studied with his father and with his uncle, and then with Muḥammad Baghayogho al-Wangarī, a scholar who was not from the Aqīt family, but originated from the Dyula, a Mande group who are both scholars and merchants. Muḥammad Baghayogho was born in Jenne, and migrated to Timbuktu along with his brother Aḥmad in his youth. He studied with Aḥmad Bābā's father, and then taught Aḥmad Bābā himself, who considered him to be his *shaykh*. He admired him tremendously, as is apparent from his description of him.[9] This description of him is not just admiration; rather his word informs us of the existence of a large library in Timbuktu, and the distribution of it to students and scholars in that city.

His library must have been inherited by his descendants, following his death in 1594; for now, more than 400 years later, a collection of manuscripts of him and his descendants exists in Timbuktu. With the title Bibliothèque Ouangari, an estimated 8,000 items are looked after by Moctar Sidi Yahya in a building on Rue Heinrich Barth,[10] just north of the Sidi Yaḥyā mosque.

Aḥmad Bābā himself had a large library, which was seized by the Moroccan forces after their occupation of Timbuktu, although his relatives had even larger libraries, as Aḥmad Bābā said: " I have the smallest number of books in my family". And, as the account states, "1,600 volumes of his were plundered".[11] Although most of the books in the libraries of Timbuktu scholars were essentials of the religion of Islam, the libraries of some of them had various books on the Arabic language, history, and other topics. In his work

Miʿrāj al-ṣuʿūd ilā nayl ḥukm mujallad al-sūd Aḥmad Bābā quoted from Ibn Khaldūn's huge "History"—*Kitāb al-ʿibar wa-dīwān al-mubtadaʾ wa ʾl-khabar fī ayyām al-ʿarab wa ʾl-Barbar, wa-manl ʿāṣarahum min dhawī ʾl-sulṭān al-akbar*, and from al-Suyūṭī's *Rafʿ shaʾn al-ḥubshān*; and it is likely that these books were in his library. And in the libraries of some Timbuktu scholars there were Arabic dictionaries; for example, in Timbuktu the historian Maḥmūd Kaʿti found for sale a manuscript of *al-Qāmūs al-muḥīṭ* [of al-Fīrūzabādī], costing 80 mithqāls, and he sought the gold to buy it from Askiya Dāwūd, ruler of the Songhay empire.[12] Towards the end of the sixteenth century the scholar Aḥmad b. Anda-Ag Muḥammad in Timbuktu ordered the copying of a manuscript in twenty-eight volumes of the dictionary *al-Muḥkam* of Ibn Sīdah (Abū ʾl-Ḥasan ʿAlī b. Ismāʿīl al-Mursī, d. 458/1066).[13]

The famous scholar Aḥmad Bābā spent the first half of his life in Timbuktu. Then after the occupation of Timbuktu by the troops of the Moroccan sultan Ḥasan Makkī Muḥammad Aḥmad in 1591 Aḥmad Bābā was expelled from Timbuktu in 1594 and transferred to Marrakesh, where he remained until 1608. For two years he was in prison in Marrakesh, and after he was released, he was forced to stay there. During his stay there he taught in the "Mosque of Nobles" (*Jāmiʿ al-Shurafāʾ*), and was asked to give many *fatwās*. Among his students were the *qāḍī* of Fez Ibn Abī Nuʿaym, the *Muftī* of Meknes Aḥmad al-Zanātī, and the celebrated Andalusian historian Shihāb al-Dīn al-Maqqarī. Because of his reputation in teaching and writing, some Moroccans even claim that he was one of their scholars. After returning to the beloved city of his birth, he continued to teach and write, but whilst he was in Marrakesh he expressed his affection and longing for his city in the following verses:

> O traveller to Gao, turn off to my city.
> Murmur my name there and greet all my dear ones,
> With scented salams from an exile who longs
> For his homeland of loved ones, companions and neighbors.[14]

Aḥmad Bābā wrote more than sixty works, many of which were of jurisprudence, and some on grammar and syntax. One of his jurisprudential works was replies about slavery entitled *Miʿrāj al-ṣuʿūd ilā nayl ḥukm mujallab al-sūd*.[15] In his reply he divided the lands of West Africa into two: lands of Muslims,[16] and lands of "unbelievers". He states that it is only permissable to enslave those who live in one of the lands of the "unbelievers". He also opposed the claim that black Africans were descendants of Ham, son of Noah, and that they became black and slaves to his other sons, Shem and Japheth, through Noah's curse. Aḥmad Bābā's statements on slavery remained remembered in West Africa for a long while after his death, and were referred to by Shaykh ʿUthmān b. Muḥammad Fodiye (or Usman ɗan Fodio), the jihādist of northern Nigeria in the early nineteenth century.

Among other scholars in Timbuktu in the same period were ʿAbd al-Raḥmān al-Saʿdī, who has been already mentioned, and another historian called Maḥmūd Kaʿti, who wrote *Taʾrīkh al-Fattāsh fī akhbār al-buldān wa'l-juyūsh wa-akābir al-nās* [plus] *wa-dhikr waqāʾiʿ al-Takrūr wa-ʿaẓāʾim al-umūr wa-tafrīq ansāb al-ʿabīd min al-aḥrār.* Three sons of his completed it, and it was revisioned by a son of his daughter called Ibn al-Mukhtār, totally finished in 1665. The book is a history of the Songhay empire from the mid-fifteenth century to near the end of the sixteenth (Maḥmūd Kaʿti died in 1592). This work also contains information on the ancient states of Mali and Ghana. The origin of the Kaʿti family was from Toledo in Spain. Maḥmūd Kaʿti's grandfather migrated from Toledo towards West Africa in the mid-1460s. This is evident from what he recorded on the last page of a manuscript of the book *al-Shifāʾ bi-taʿrīf ḥuqūq al-Muṣṭafā* by *Qāḍī* ʿIyāḍ, where the migrant mentioned the purchase of it in the oasis of Touat in 872 [A.H.= 1468], "two months after arriving there from our town of Toledo, the capital of the Goths, and now we are on our way to the land of the blacks (*bilād al-sūdān*), asking of God Most High that He should grant us repose there".[17] It appears from that that he considered the zone of Timbuktu to be an attractive place for one in need of relaxation.

As is now clear, Timbuktu was a home for scholars in the fifteenth and sixteenth centuries; and indeed it remained so down to the twentieth century, and it was still an attractive city for scholars from the Sahara and from north-west Africa. One of the most significant migrants to Timbuktu in the twentieth century was Aḥmad b. al-Mubārak al-Tikinī, known as Abū 'l-Aʿrāf. His town of origin was Gulimīm in Darʿa in southern Morocco. He was both a merchant and a scholar, loving books and collecting a large number of manuscripts after his arrival to Timbuktu in 1907. After he died in 1955, they were inherited by one of his sons, and around 1973 most of them were donated to the Aḥmad Bābā Center [CEDRAB] which had just been founded. As for Abū 'l-Aʿrāf himself, he wrote approximately forty works, most of which were versifications or abridgements of works written by others. He himself wrote an important original work, ressembling one that Aḥmad

Bābā wrote; that is *Izālat al-rayb wa 'l-shakk wa'l-tafrīṭ fī dhikr al-'ulamā' al-mu'allifīn min ahl al-Takrūr wa 'l-Ṣaḥrā' wa-Shinqīṭ*. It is like a supplement to *Nayl al-ibtihāj,* since its composition was about three hundred years after what Aḥmad Bābā wrote, and it contains biographies of scholars who lived in that long intermediary period. As for "Takrūr", what is meant by it is the whole lands of Muslims in West Africa. A millenium ago, it was originally the name of a state on the bank of the river Senegal.

Among the scholars in the second half of the twentieth century was Aḥmad Bābēr al-Arawānī, who died in 1997. He also wrote a work on biographies of scholars: *al-Sa'āda al-abadiyya fī 'l-ta'rīf bi-'ulamā' Tinbuktu al-bahiyya* . Furthermore he wrote some historical works, for example: *Jawāhir al-ḥisān fī akhbār al-sūdān,*[18] and *Ta'rīkh Azawād,* which is an edition with further material of a history of the Barābīsh tribe by Maḥmūd b. Daḥmān, Azawad being a Saharan area between Timbuktu and Arawān [Araouan], a trading town, and the birthplace of Aḥmad Bābēr.

As for conservation of Arabic manuscripts in Timbuktu, there is a number of private libraries, and a public library—the Centre de Documentation et de Recherches historiques Ahmad Baba (CEDRAB), set up in 1973, following a recommendation sent to the government of Mali from a 1967 conference of [Experts on] Arabic sources of African history,[19] held in Timbuktu through the Unesco. One of the most important private libraries is the "Memorial Library of Mamma Haidara", run by Abdul-Kader ['Abd al-Qādir] Ḥaidara, who inherited some 5,000 manuscripts from his father, who had died in 1981. Then, in the year 2000, a building was set up to preserve the manuscripts, with a financial grant from the Mellon Foundation of America [sought by Henry Louis Gates of Harvard University], and Abdul-Kader cataloged the manuscripts, and the catalog was published by the Al-Furqan Foundation Islamic Heritage, London, 2000.

In Timbuktu another library building was set up in 2003. That was the "Fondo Ka'ti", administered by Ismael Diadié Haidara, who collected more than 2,000 manuscripts from family members living outside of Timbuktu, and brought them to Timbutu for conservation before 1999. Because of the links of the Ka'ti family with Spain, the government of Spain eventually provided a grant for building a center for conservation of the manuscripts.[20] Many of these manuscripts are truly ancient: e.g. a copy of the Qur'ān, copied in Istanbul in 827/ 1423–4. Another is a 2-volume copy of the book *al-Shifa' bi-ta'rīf ḥuqūq al-Muṣṭafā* by Qāḍī 'Iyāḍ, in a Maghribī calligraphy, copied some time before 872/ 1467, the year of its purchase in the

Touat oasis by ʿAlī b. Ziyād al-Qūṭī, ancestor of the historian Maḥmūd Kaʿti, as mentioned before. Another manuscript of this library is a copy of *Dalāʾil al-khayrāt*—or something like it, though the distinguishing feature of it is the recording of events of the sixteenth century in its margins: among such is a great rainfall in one year, and the much agriculture following that. In another margin is an extraordinary event, as follows:

> In the year 991, in God's goodly month of Rajab, more than half way through the night, the stars in the sky flew around, as if fire had been kindled in the whole sky—east and west, north and south. It became mighty blazes illuninating land, and people were extremely alarmed. It continued until after lightness.

Also in the Fondo Kaʿti [library] are many well-known writings for teaching Arabic, studying jurisprudence, and other Islamic sciences; *e.g.* the *Alfiyya* of Ibn Mālik, *al-Muqaddima al-Ājurrūmiyya*,[21] *al-ʿIshrīniyyāt* of al-Fāzāzī, and *al-Maqāmāt* of al-Ḥarīrī; the *Mukhtaṣar* of Khalīl [b. Isḥāq], the *Risāla* of al-Qayrawānī, the *Ṣaḥīḥ* of al-Bukhārī, and the *Tafsīr al-Jalālayn* of al-Suyūtī.

Certainly in Timbuktu there are many other libraries. One of the best known is the library of the Imam of the Jingere Bēr mosque, the contents of which were once preserved in an underground store room, and now the Imam's son is reviving it in a room of the Imam's house, although the manuscripts need conservation and cataloging. As regards all the libraries of Timbuktu, Abdul Kader Ḥaidara recorded a list of them in a French-language article in 1999.[22] More can also be seen in the following chapter: 5: The Islamic Manuscript Heritage of Timbuktu.

It is clear that Timbuktu was, and still is, a homeland for scholars, and one of the most important places in sub-Saharan Africa for Islamic knowledge.

Chapter Five

The Islamic Manuscript Heritage of Timbuktu

It is said in the chronicles of Timbuktu (written in the seventeenth century) that the origins of Timbuktu go back to around the year 1100, when some nomads established a summer camp a few miles away from the river Niger as a base from which they could pasture and water their camels during the hottest weather. Hence, Timbuktu's position proved strategic for commerce.This camp site gradually attracted people who settled there and turned it into a permanent dwelling place. It was situated at the junction of the dry Sahara and the lush central valley of the river Niger, a waterway that constituted an easy pathway for transporting goods to and from the more tropical regions of West Africa. Over the early centuries of its existence Timbuktu rapidly attracted settlers, in the form of merchants, and then Muslim scholars, from Saharan oases such as Walata, Touat, Ghadames, and the Fezzan, and from the southern reaches of Morocco. Ghadames traders played an important role in Timbuktu trade from the fifteenth to the nineteenth century. Ghadames was a gateway to Tripoli and for routes leading to Egypt, while to the south it also established commercial ties with Kano. Touat was also a trade entrepot, with routes radiating out to Fez, Algiers and Tunis in the north, and Gao, Agades, and Katsina in the south.

Timbuktu's importance as a center of commerce is vividly illustrated by its first appearance on a European map in 1375. This was a map draw for the Catalan ruler Charles V by a Jewish cartographer of Majorca, hinting no doubt at the role played by Jewish merchants in trans-Saharan trade. A quarter of a century earlier Timbuktu had been visited by the extraordinary Muslim traveler from Tangier, Ibn Baṭṭūṭa, who found there the grave of an Andalusian poet, Abū Isḥāq Ibrāhīm al-Sāḥilī, who had accompanied the ruler of Mali, Mansa Mūsā, upon his return from the *ḥajj* in 1325. Timbuktu at that time was part of the great medieval empire of Mali, and it was this ruler, Mansa Musa, who ordered the construction of the Great Mosque—Jingere Ber—and the Andalusian al-Sāḥilī, who oversaw the actual construction.

The building of a great congregational mosque clearly established Timbuktu as an Islamic city, and over the next two centuries many Muslim scholars were attracted to settle in it, so that by the mid-fifteenth century Timbuktu had become a major center of Islamic teaching.

Many of the scholars settled in the north-eastern quarter of the city, called Sankore, where another large mosque was built and named after the quarter. The Sankore mosque was also a location for teaching Islamic texts, though individual scholars also taught their students in, or near, their own homes. It was in these homes of scholars that the establishment of libraries took place. Some of these personal libraries were evidently quite large. Timbuktu's most celebrated scholar, Ahmad Baba (1564–1627) claimed that his library contained 1,600 volumes and that it was the smallest library of any of his family—his family. the Aqīt, being the leading scholarly family that provided the city with *qaḍīs* throughout the sixteenth century. Ahmad Baba was, of course, part of the Timbuktu teaching tradition. His primary shaykh was a certain Muḥammad Baghayogho, a Mande Dyula scholar who migrated to Timbuktu from Jenne. To give you an idea of the teaching tradition, let me quote part of a biography of Muḥammad Baghayogho, recorded by his pupil Aḥmad Bābā in his famous biographical dictionary *Nayl al-ibtihāj*[1] (a supplement to Ibn Farḥūn's dictionary of Mālikī scholars *al-Dībāj al-mudhahhab fī Maʿrifat Aʿyān ʿUlamāʾal-Madh'hab)*:

> Our shaykh and our [source of] blessing, the jurist, and accomplished scholar, a pious and ascetic man of God, who was among the finest of God's righteous servants and practising scholars. He was a man given by nature to goodness and benign intent, guileless, and naturally disposed to goodness, believing in people to such an extent that all men were virtually equal in his sight, so well did he think of them and absolve

> them of wrongdoing. Moreover, he was constantly attending to people's needs, even at cost to himself, becoming distressed at their misfortunes, mediating their disputes, and giving counsel. Add to this his love of learning, and his devotion to teaching—in which pursuit he spent his days—his close association with men of learning, and his own utter humility, his lending of his most rare and precious books in all fields without asking for them back again, no matter what discipline they were in. Thus it was that he lost a [large] portion of his books—may God shower His beneficence upon him for that! Sometimes a student would come to his door asking for a book, and he would give it to him without even knowing who the student was. In this matter he was truly astonishing, doing this for the sake of God Most High, despite his love for books and [his zeal in] acquiring them, whether by purchase or copying. One day I came to him asking for books on grammar, and he hunted through his library and brought me everything he could find on the subject.[2]

It is clear from this that the man himself possessed a considerable library, to which any aspiring scholar could have access.What kind of books would such a library have contained? First and foremost, it would have contained the texts that were to be taught to his students: commentaries on the Qur'ān, books of *ḥadīth*, theological treatises in the Sunnī Ashʿarī tradition, and works of Mālikī jurisprudence (*fiqh*), such as *al-Muwaṭṭaʾ* of Mālik b. Anas, the *Mudawwana* of Saḥnūn,[3] the *Risāla* of Ibn Abī Zayd al-Qayrawānī, and the *Mukhtaṣar* of Khalīl b. Isḥāq, with some of its many commentaries; and works on Arabic grammar, such as the *Alfiyya* of Ibn Mālik and the *Mulḥat al-iʿrāb* of al-Ḥarīrī. But Timbuktu scholarship went beyond the teaching of basic texts. We know, for example that Aḥmad Bābā had access to the great History of Ibn Khaldūn (*Kitāb al-ʿibar*), a work which he quotes from in one of his writings. In the same work he also quotes passages from al-Suyūṭī's *Rafʿ shaʾn al-Ḥubshān*, a less than commonly circulating work.

Indeed, there was clearly an important trade in books in sixteenth century Timbuktu. This is clear from the account of Leo Africanus (al-Ḥasan b. Muḥammad al-Wazzān al-Zayyatī), who visited Timbuktu in the early years of that century and observed: "Many manuscript books coming from Barbary are sold. Such sales are more profitable than any other goods". Not only were manuscripts imported to Timbuktu, both from North Africa and Egypt, but scholars going on pilgrimage studied in both Mecca and, on the way back, in Cairo, and often copied texts to add to their own libraries. There was also an active copying industry in Timbuktu itself. One amazing piece of evidence for this is a work that the scholar Aḥmad b. Anda Ag-Muḥammad had copied for himself in the late sixteenth century.

That work was an Arabic dictionary, *al-Muḥkam* of the Andalusian scholar Ibn Sīdah (d. 1066) and the copying of the full work, running to twenty-eight volumes, was completed in Timbuktu in April 1574. What is interesting about these volumes—four of which I examined in Morocco over thirty years ago—is that their colophons throw some light on the copying industry of sixteenth-century Timbuktu, thus confirming the interest in book collection and library building. The colophons name the copyists, the person for whom they were copied, and who provided the blank paper for them, the dates of beginning and ending the copying of each volume, and the amount paid to the copyists. The colophons, in essence, constitute a labor contract. Two of the (double) volumes contain a second colophon, in which another person records that he verified the accuracy of the copying , and records what he was paid. The copyist received 1 mithqal of gold (4.238 gr./0.15 [3/20] oz) per volume, and the 'proof-reader' half that amount.

It would appear, from the evidence provided in these various colophons, that manuscript copying was, truly, a professionalized business. Compensation was paid by legal contract, and it would seem that both the copyist and the 'proof-reader' (himself also a professional copyist) worked full time to complete their contracted tasks; the copyist was copying some 7.5 ff or 142 lines of text per day, while the 'proof-reader' was going through the material at the rate of 9 ff (or 171 lines) of text per day.

We know less about whether or not there were public libraries in sixteenth century Timbuktu. One of the rulers of the Songhay empire, that incorporated Timbuktu within it in 1468, Askiya *al-ḥājj* Muḥammad b. Abī Bakr (reg. 1493–1528) made an endowment of 60 *juz*ʾ [equivalent to two complete copies] of the Qurʾān to the Great Mosque [*Jingere Ber*] of Timbuktu, and it is said that a later ruler, Askiya Dāwūd (1549–1583), set up public libraries in his state, though no trace of them has yet been discovered.

What has survived, however, is the private collection [or parts of it] of one of the two great chroniclers of Timbuktu, Maḥmūd Kaʿti, now looked after by one of his descendants in Timbuktu, who re-assembled it from various branches of the Kaʿti family who had inherited it over generations. I was privileged to see a number of items from this library when I was in Timbuktu in August 1999.[4] I was truly amazed to see that the copying of some of these manuscripts went back to the sixteenth, and even in some cases the fifteenth, century. For example, I saw a beautiful copy of the Qur'ān in a fine eastern script with a copying date equivalent to 1420 AD (823 AH). The final page was, in fact, written in Turkish, and recorded the fact that the copy had been dedicated as a *waqf* in the name of a woman entitled *Sharīfa* Khadīja Khānum. How this manuscript got to Timbuktu we do not know. Perhaps it was purchased by Maḥmūd Ka'ti, or some member of his family whilst on pilgrimage.

Another very old and very beautiful manuscript is a copy of the *Kitab al-Shifā'' bi-ta'rīf ḥuqūq al-Mussṭafā* by the eleventh-century Moroccan scholar, *Qāḍī* 'Iyāḍ. Although we do not know the date of copying, a note at he end of volume 1 tells us that it was purchased in 1468. What is truly surprising is that it was purchased in an oasis of the Sahara by a man migrating from Toledo in Spain to "the land of the Blacks" (*bilād al-sūdān*), hoping to find repose there. The note reads as follows:

> I bought this illuminated book called *al-Shifā'* [*bi-ta'rīf ḥuqūq al-Muṣṭafā*] by the *Qadi* 'Iyāḍ from its first owner Muḥammad b. 'Umar in a [legally] valid sale, for the sum of 45 *mithqāls* of gold in cash [about 3.5 oz], paid in its entirety to the one from whom it was purchased with the witness of our companions. This took place two months after our arrival in Touat coming from our city of Toldeo, capital of the Goths. And we are now on our way to the land of the blacks (*bilad al-sudan*), asking of God Most High that He should grant us repose there.
>
> I, the servant of his Lord, 'Alī b. Ziyād al-Qūṭī, wrote [this] in Muḥarram of the year 873 of the Prophetic *hijra*. [July–August 1468][5]

The writer of the note, and purchaser of the manuscript turns out to be the grandfather of Maḥmūd Ka'ti, so evidently the male ancestry of the family was from central Spain, and appears to clain Visigoth origins. However they settled in West Africa and married locally, since Mahmūd Ka'ti himself uses a *nisba* [ethnic label] that relates him to the Soninke people [Wa'kuri], and it is possible that he was related in marriage to the ruling dynasty, the Askiyas, of the Songhay empire, whose male ancestry was also Soninke.

Another very fascinating item in the collection is prized not for its physical beauty or its content, but for the notes written in the margins. The identity of the book is not known, as it lacks its opening folios. All we can say is that it is a devotional work seeking God's mercy by invoking the names of the four great imams, founders of the *madh'habs* of jurisprudence and some other great figures. But Mahmūd Kaʿti used the manuscript's wide margins, not to comment on the text, but to record certain local events; it is as if it were his diary. Why he used the manuscript for this purpose we do not know, but it may be that because the price of paper in sixteenth-century Timbuktu was high (being mainly imported from Europe), he just decided to use the blank space to record fragments of history. It is not uncommon for owners on manuscripts to record notes on the title page of amanuscript, just as American Christians used to use the first blank page of a copy of the Bible to record family matters.

His marginal notes record a wide variety of events, most of which would otherwise be unknown to us. Here are some examples:

> In that year God caused prices to fall, rains were abundant, and wells filled up. As soon as rain began to fall, people began to plant, and God facilitated harvesting of the crop. He sent successive rains to His servants following the year 910 [1504–5], and people continued thus for five years.

Here, then, is a remarkable piece of climatological data, that no other known source gives us. Another cosmological event is recorded towards the end of the century:

> In the year 991 in God's month of Rajab the Goodly [August 1583], after half the night had passed, stars flew around the sky as if fire had been kindled in the whole sky—east, west, north, and south. It became a mighty flame lighting up the earth, and people were extremely disturbed about that. It continued until after dawn.
>
> Recorded by the humble servant of his Lord, Alfa Katʿi Maḥmūd b. ʿAlī b. al-Mutawakkil bi'llāh b. Ziyād al-Qūṭī al-Waʿqarī in the year 991 [1583].

Here again is a unique piece of information—as I would interpret it, a meteor shower—that is of a nature that would not lead it to be included in a chronicle [It is certainly not in Maḥmūd Kaʿti's chronicle]. Chronicles generally deal mainly, though not exclusively, with political events.

Other events recorded in these margins include a wedding, the death of a scholar, and brief statements of some of Maḥmūd Kaʿti's journeys in the area. There are many more pages with marginal notes in this manuscript, but I did not have time to examine or photograph more than a very few. It is our hope that the Institute for the Study of Islamic Thought in Africa (ISITA), which we set up at Northwestern University in January 2001,[6] will be able to fund the taking of many more images (photographic or digital), and to sponsor seminars of interpretation that would include Timbuktu scholars and other international specialists. We hope, too, to be able to help the curator of the collection, Ismael Diadié Haidara, to have the collection scientifically preserved, and already a special building has been constructed to house the 3,000 manuscripts that make up the full collection.[7]

The Kaʿti library [Fondo Kaʿti], however, is not the only valuable library in Timbuktu. A collection of 5,000 Arabic manuscripts was inherited by Abdul-Kadir Ḥaidara from his father, and that has now been housed in a new library building funded by an American foundation through Henry Lewis Gates of Harvard University, and the Al-Furqan Foundation has already published a catalog of it. There are, indeed, some twenty private manuscript libraries in Timbuktu.

The largest collection of Arabic manuscripts, however, is a public one in Timbuktu at the Ahmad Baba Center for Documentation and Historical Research, generally known by its abbreviated French title as CEDRAB.[8] The origins of that center go back to a meeting that I was privileged to attend in 1967. When UNESCO was beginning to plan its multi-volume history of Africa, it convened a "Meeting of Experts" in Timbuktu to examine the range of Arabic sources for African history. At the conclusion of the meeting, chaired by Najm al-Din Bammate [a Unesco official of Afghan origin], a resolution was passed calling on the government of Mali to establish a center for the preservation of Arabic manuscripts in Timbuktu. Some years later in 1973, after funding had been raised [principally from Kuwait] the center was built, and soon manuscripts were being obtained, either by gift or purchase, from private libraries in Timbuktu. It developed and expanded considerably after the appointment in the late 1970s of Dr Mahmoud Zoubeir, who directed CEDRAB for some 15 years until he was made ambassador of Mali to Saudi Arabia, and in 1999 became a counsellor on religious affairs to the president of Mali.

CEDRAB now contains some 20,000 manuscripts, ranging from single-page archival documents to large scholarly tomes. A handlist of the first 9,000 items has been published by the Al-Furqan Islamic Heritage Foundation, London.[9] The great majority of the items preserved at the Centre Ahmad Baba are of local authorship, though some non-local items have been acquired if they have some historical or aesthetic interest. Among the latter we may note a beautiful illuminated copy of *al-Shifāʾ bi-taʿrīf ḥuqūq al-Muṣṭafā* of *Qāḍī* ʿIyāḍ (no. 3178), penned in Morocco and one volume (in 80ff.) of the *Wafāyāt al-aʿyān* of Ibn Khallikān in the hand of Aḥmad Bābā, copied by him in Marrakesh in 1599 (no. 3866). Almost all the items are in the Arabic language, though the index does record the existence of a letter in Tamacheq and several poems and letters in the Songhay language—the only examples of this language written in the Arabic script so far preserved, to the best of my knowledge.

It is difficult to do justice to the richness of the collection in a single limited chapter such as this, but it may be worthwhile to indicate some of the principal categories of materials and to give illustrative examples of some of them. There are two broad categories of material:

(1) Items of a 'literary' character—religious treatises, chronicles, poems, all of which (or most of which) may be attributed to an author.

(2) Items of a documentary character, including letters, and commercial and legal documents. Between these two categories come a large number of items that are in one sense documents, and in another sense—in that they are written by scholarly authors—works belonging to a literary tradition. These are the *fatwās*—both individual ones on specific topics and collected volumes—and *rasāʾil* ['letters'] and *ajwiba* ['replies'] , often on quite specific topics but addressed to particular individuals or groups. There are a dozen or so major collections of *fatwās* at CEDRAB, totalling over 1,800 ff. Some of these are collections of the legal opinions of a particular scholar, whilst others are more diverse collections of opinions of the scholars of the region as a whole. Most of the collections by single individuals are, in fact, by scholars of Mauritanian origin, though the major one is by the late nineteenth to early twentieth century Kunta scholar *Shaykh* Bay b. Sīdī ʿUmar al-Kuntī (1865–1920+)which runs to some 488 ff. in nine volumes (nos. 118–126). There are three copies of the major collection of the *fatwās* of the scholars of 'al-Takrūr'—*al-*

ʿAmal al-mashkūr fī jamʿ nawāzil ʿulamāʾ al-Takrūr by al-Muṣṭafā b. Aḥmad al-Ghallāwī (nos. 521, 1031, 5346).

As a matter of interest, here is a short list of some of the topics dealt with in these *fatwās* and *responsa*, mainly dating from the nineteenth and early twentieth centuries:

i) On dwelling with the Christians
ii) On lost camels
iii) On ritual purity.
iv) On a wife's rejection of her husband's authority (*nushūz*).
v) On whether is it permissible to eat with a man who fails to perform *wuḍūʾ* without valid reason.[10]
vi) On a slave who committed a crime against a free boy.
vii) On the purchasing of plundered goods.
viii) On division of inheritance.
ix) On cutting down trees in order to feed goats.
x) On a man and woman who befriended one another, claiming that they were related through milk kinship.
xi) On a married couple who were told after many years of marriage that they were related through milk kinship.
xii) On a man who married a women without anyone telling him she was within the prohibited degrees of marriage.
xiii) On the failure of women to observe wearing of a veil (*ḥijāb*).

These and other *fatwās* will eventually help us to better understand the nature of social and economic issues in the Timbuktu region in the nineteenth and early twentieth centuries, and how Islamic law regulated them.

As regards purely religious issues, there is relatively little writing, since all the Muslims of the Timbuktu region are Ashʿarī Sunnis and adherents of the Mālikī *madh'hab.* The one exception is the conflictual literature over Sufism. Prior to the nineteenth century the only Sufi *ṭarīqa* in the region was the Qādiriyya. By the middle of the nineteenth century the new Tijāniyya *ṭarīqa* [following the teachings of Aḥmad al-Tijānī, who died in Morocco in 1815] had been introduced into the broader region, and gained adherents. The two *ṭarīqa*s became rivals, especially since they were also associated with political leaders. Some also rallied against Aḥmad al-Tijānī's spiritual claims, and his assertion of the uniqueness of his *ṭarīqa*, and his refusal to allow his followers to have any association with any other Sufi *shaykh*.

In conclusion, here are projects I am involved in to perpetuate the Timbuktu library legacy, and make the city's intellectual heritage more widely accessible. The first of these, which I initiated a decade ago, is called "Arabic Literature of Africa", or ALA for short.[11] The object of it is to produce a series of published volumes—a total of about eight—as a guide to the Muslim writers of sub-Saharan Africa and their writings, principally in Arabic, as the title suggests, but also including anything they also wrote in African languages that were, before the twentieth century, written using the Arabic script. Writers are grouped together according to their relationships to one another; family, ethnic group, city, Sufi *ṭarīqa*, etc. Each author is presented through a brief biography; then his/her works are listed alphabetically, with indications of where manuscript copies are to be found. Hence, a researcher will eventually be able to trace any work written in Arabic in sub-Saharan [and Saharan] Africa. The first two volumes, originally published in English, will soon be republished in Arabic.[12] The first deals with the Sudan down to 1900, and was prepared by my colleague Professor Sean O'Fahey of the University of Bergen [Norway]. The second, which I prepared, covers Nigeria and Chad. Later I prepared volume 4, published in 2003 in some 814 pages. It covers the Timbuktu tradition and the rest of Mali, as well as Senegal, Guinea, Niger and Ghana. Professor O'Fahey is preparing volume 3 covering Ethiopia, Eritrea, Somalia in Part I, and the Swahili coast of East Africa [in which he lists writings in Swahili as well as Arabic] in Part II. Soon we shall begin work on the Sudan in the twentieth century, and later I hope to work with other colleagues to produce a volume on Mauritania.

The other project, which I am also carrying out jointly with Professor O'Fahey (an Adjunct Professor at Northwestern University[13]) is the Institute for the Study of Islamic Thought in Africa (ISITA), which we inaugurated in January 2001. On detailed information on ISITA (and ALA), see Appendix 1 below.

As regards our first objective, concentration will be on the libraries of Timbuktu. We hope to help library owners to preserve their manuscripts scientifically, and to digitize them so that the contents of the library can be more widely available, and accessible to researchers without actually having to handle the manuscripts themselves. At the same time we shall help produce computerized catalogs of the contents of the libraries to facilitate research. We shall work closely with the forthcoming International Association for the Conservation of Arabic Manuscripts, an institution planned at a symposium [the "Ink Road"] in Mali in August 2002.We also wish to hold international seminars at Northwestern University to bring together scholars to analyze, and in some cases to translate, some of the more significant manuscripts, especially those of historical interest. Later we hope to do similar things for libraries in Nigeria, the Sudan, Zanzibar and other African countries.

ISITA has already had some senior African fellows in residence, and in May 2001 we held an international colloquium on the theme :" Libraries and the transmission of Islamic knowledge in Africa", the proceedings of which will soon be in press. In academic year 2001–2 we had both senior fellows and, in Spring 2002, junior African fellows to work on the theme: "Muslim commentaries on the State", with special emphasis on the responses of African Muslims to the colonial state.

We hope that this institute will be a permanent feature of Northwestern's intellectual life, and that Islamic thought (beginning with Africa) will become an integral part of our teaching curriculum. We hope, too, to enlighten the general public as to the role that Islam has played in African societies, and to the fact that much of Africa has enjoyed literacy and an intellectual life—matters that may help to erase some of the unfortunate stereotypes about Africa that have been current, and in many cases exacerbated by racist thinking. Timbuktu will cease to be seen just as a legendary fantasy, and will be recognized for what it really was—a spiritual and intellectual jewel inspired by the Islamic faith.

Part III

The Arab World

Chapter Six

Arabic as the Latin of Africa

Arabic is what I often describe as "the Latin of Africa", since it has played a role in West Africa (and some other parts of Africa) over the past millenium as Latin did in Europe in the Medieval era.

Latin was the native language of the Romans, who occupied Jerusalem and many areas of Europe in the first millenium A.D. Romans, who had adopted Christianity, had translated the essential New Testament into Latin. Hence, in European areas that they occupied, Christianity was broadly adopted, and those converted Christians had to learn how to read Latin in order to follow up on their religion. Many Europeans who did so, then learned the language well enough to be able to do their own writing—for the first time—in Latin. In fact, Latin remained the essential language of Christianity for all those who followed the Roman expression of that religion; i.e. Catholicism. Also, after the first millenium, many Europeans adopted the script of the Latin language to write their own native languages—English being one of the most obvious adopters of the Latin script.

Within a decade after the prophet Muḥammad, not only had Arabs of the peninsula [now Saudi Arabia] accepted Islam and the role of the caliph, but the original forces sent from Mecca were overtaken by a large number of the converted bedouins, many of whom, after converting Arabs in the north-east of the penninsula, decided to move beyond Arab-inhabited territories and take over areas in what is now Iraq. They then went on into what is now Iran, and also towards the Mediterranean Sea, taking over what are now Lebanon, Syria and Palestine, all of which had been parts of the Byzantine empire. Those areas became elements of the Islamic Empire, and in Syria many Christians remained Christians; though from Damascus a Christian leader in 636 contacted Caliph 'Umar with a list of conditions upon themselves as being *Ahl al-dhimma* ('protected people'), remaining Christians, but respecting Muslims.[1] The Arabic language became the native language of all those areas (except Iran), and the majority—but not all—of inhabitants adopted Islam as their religion.

Early in the year 640 A.D., Arab forces moved into the African continent, most of the north of which was then under Byzantine rule. They moved over what is now called the Gaza Strip and into Egypt, taking over all the northern areas of it, and later establishing contact with the 'Christian' rulers of Nubia with an agreement on commercial exchanges.[2] After three years in Egypt they passed into what is now Libya and took control over much of it, then moving westwards again into the area called Ifrīqiya, which is now that state of Tunisia, fighting against the Byzantines, and in 670 set up a Muslim military city called Qayrawān. Soon afterwards, they moved to occupy other territories farther west, and by the end of the seventh century had taken over all lands of North Africa to about 150 miles south of the Mediterranean Sea, and all the way from the Red Sea to the Atlantic. Arabic became the dominant language of all such territories after decades, though Berber continued also to be spoken by some for centuries in the western regions; and, of course, Islam became the religion adopted by the conquered human beings. No occupation was made — at least in the early centuries— of the Sahara, or of lands to the south of it. However, in the ninth century North African Muslims (Arab-Berbers) began to move across the Sahara to do trade with settled populations of the Sahel—the southern 'coast' of the Sahara—the desert being seen as huge and as difficult to move through as an ocean; hence where the true desert ceased to be just sand, and began to grow small amounts of bushes and grass, it became known as the Sahel (*al-Sāḥil*) or 'coast'. Although in the desert only a small number of inhabitants dwelt — in water and growth regions called oases—more human beings dwelt in parts of the Sahel region, many having moved from their Saharan homes when the real desert came into existence [by 200 B.C.].

In the ninth century many camels were brought into North Africa from Asia, and hence North African Muslims began to use them to ride, or to carry trading items, going across the Sahara.[3] The areas they first reached in the Sahel of West Africa were (1) Ancient Ghana, a state in what is now partly southern Mauritania and northern Mali. and (2) the 'Middle Niger' —the region where the river Niger had flowed north to the Sahel and then eastwards to Gao, and (3) the zone of the Kanem just north of Lake Chad, following a route that Romans had once used to the middle of the Sahara when they occupied what is now Libya.

One of the main original activities of the Arab Muslim traders was to seize both men and women as slaves; and this may be one of the reasons for persuading some local populations to convert to Islam, so that, as Muslims, they might remain free, for it has always been illegal (*ḥarām*) for a Muslim to be enslaved by a Muslim—though later some non-Muslim West Africans captured Muslims and sold them to America as slaves.[4] This may have been one kind of encouragement for Sahel folk to convert to Islam.

. Despite not being controlled by Arabs, such Africans who converted to Islam soon learned the Arabic language, so that they could read the Qurʾān and properly offer verses of it in their five daily prayers.[5] Thus becoming acquainted with Arabic for religion, many sub-Saharan Africans soon adopted Arabic as their language of writing, after learning to read it in the Qurʾān, though it did not become their main language of speech, as it had become in North Africa and the Middle East when being ruled by Arabs. West African Muslims continued to rule themselves, but often established good contacts with the Arab (-Islamic) world.

On account of this, I like to call Arabic "the Latin of Africa", for in Europe, in the first millenium A.D., many areas were conquered by the Romans, and their inhabitants became Christians. Romans had translated the New Testament into their language of Latin, so converted Europeans came to know the Latin language, and used it also as their language of writing for several centuries. Such Europeans adopted the Latin script for the writing of their own native languages; and, similarly, many (but certainly not all) West African Muslims eventually adopted the Arabic script to write in their own native languages; e.g. Kanuri, Fulani, Hausa, Yoruba, Wolof, and Songhay. In sub-Saharan West Africa, over coming centuries, Arabic writings became more and more, covering many different topics. One of the earliest uses of Arabic was for the registration of buried rulers (and relatives) on tombstones, especially close to Gao, on the R. Niger in the Sahel: e.g.

> This is the tomb of the king who gave victory to the religion of Allāh and entrusted himself to Allāh: Abū ʿAbd Allāh b. ʿAbd Allāh b. Zāghī — God's mercy and foregiveness, and His favor, be upon him. He died on Monday, 1 Muḥarram, at the beginning of year 494/ 6 November 1100. May God have mercy upon

> whomever reads [this] and calls for mercy and foregiveness for himwelf.; Amen — Lord of the Worlds.

This, and many others, has been published in a fine recent book by Paulo de Moraes Farias, *Arabic Medieval Inscriptions from the Republic of Mali.*[6]

Many other types of writing came into existence, especially in Timbuktu, in the fifteenth to sixteenth century, and in Kano, Sokoto, and Bornu in the northern area of modern Nigeria in the eighteenth to nineteenth century.

In Timbuktu there was writing of biographies and local history. Aḥmad Bābā (1556–1627) wrote a total of about seventy works in Arabic, including some items on legal matters and some poetry. One of his most celebrated works was a biographical dictionary, *Nayl al-Ibtihāj*, the supplement of such a work by the Mālikī Arabian Ibn Farḥūn (d. 1397).[7] This work gave information on relative scholars of his and many others, including some in north-west Africa, where he spent more than a decade, being exiled by the Moroccan force that occupied Timbuktu in 1591–2. One of the men whom he wrote about was a Dyula [Mande] scholar from Jenne, who came to Timbuktu in the mid-sixteenth century and became a teacher of Aḥmad Bābā; that was Muḥammad Baghayogho, who was also owner of a large Arabic manuscript library. On him he said:

> Our shaykh and our [source of] blessing, the jurist, and accomplished scholar, a pious and ascetic man of God, who was among the finest of God's righteous servants and practising scholars. He was a man given by nature to goodness and benign intent, guileless, and naturally disposed to goodness, believing in people to such an extent that all men were virtually equal in his sight, so well did he think of them and absolve them of wrongdoing. Moreover, he was constantly attending to people's needs, even at cost to himself, becoming distressed at their misfortunes, mediating their disputes, and advising them to have love for learning and to closely follow his teaching. He spent most of his time doing this, with affection for those concerned, with his own utter humility, helping them and caring for them, and his lending them of the most rare and precious books without searching for them again, no matter what discipline they were in. Thus it was that he lost a [large] portion of his books—may God shower His beneficence upon

> him for that! Sometimes a student would come to the door of his house and send him a note listing a the book he was looking for, and he would take the book out of his library and despatch it to him, without even knowing who the student was. In this matter he was truly astonishing, doing this for the sake of God Most High, despite his love for books and his zeal in acquiring them, whether by purchase or copying. One day I [Aḥmad Bābā] came to him asking for books on grammar, and he hunted through his library and brought me everything he could find on the subject.[8]

Northern Nigeria also had historians who wrote in Arabic. ʿUthmān b. Muḥammad Fūdī (in Hausa: Usmanu ɗan Fodio) (1754–1814) wrote about his own *jihād* efforts to take control over the Hausa peoples of Sokoto and other north-western regions: *Bayān wujūb al-hijra ʿala ʾl-ʿibād.*[9] His brother ʿAbd Allah in 1813 wrote *Tazyīn al-waraqāt bi-jamʿ baʿḍ mā lī min al-abyāt*, ['The decoration of pages through putting together some of my verses'] That was an account of that *jihād*, with poems of his related to it. It opens:

> It came to my mind that I should collect some of the verses which I composed in praise of the shaykhs and in elegizing them, and in thanksgiving for the favors which God has bestowed upon us through them before our *hijra* and concerning the battles which took place during the Holy War after the *hijra.*[10]

Usmanu ɗan Fodio's son—and governing successor—Muḥammad Bello—also wrote a history of that *jihād*, together with other information on neighboring regions: *Infāq al-Maysūr fī taʾrīkh bilād al-Takrūr*['An Outlay of the Successful—on the history of the lands of Takrūr', i.e. Muslim West Africa].[11] Another *jihād* volume is on what happened to Kano: *Taqyīd Akhbār Jamāʿat al-Shuyūkh alladhīna bi-Kanū wa-mā jarā baynahum wa-bayna ʾl-Ṭāghūt al-Walī min al-ḥurūb*['Registration of the News of all the *shaykhs* (rulers) in Kano, and what occurred between them and battles between the neighboring Tempters'] by Muḥammad b. Ṣāliḥ, the *qāḍī* of Kano, writing in 1868.

Although most Arabic writing was in prose, some authors also wrote poetry—much on religious matters—and some of it was written in their own African languages, but using the Arabic script for such writing. One of the most celebrated of such poets was Nānā Asmāʾu, the daughter of Usman ∂an Fodiyo, who wrote poems in Arabic, and in Hausa, and in Fulani—a minimum of 11–41 vv., with a huge one of 316vv. All, in one way or another, expressed religious thoughts and prayers. Here are the first verses of a Fulani poem of hers about the victory of Caliph ʿAliyu, the son of Muḥammad Bello:

We give thanks to God, who has helped us to overcome the enemy.
  Let us continue with our efforts.
Thank Him, for God increases the blessings
  on each person who gives Him thanks.
Δan Mari, the obdurate, has been taught a lesson
  and he and Mayaªi have retreated in disgrace.
Their forces, including their cavalry, were put to flight
  and no one knows where they are.
They did not halt at Maradi; they have gone into hiding
  in a state of shock.
They know they tried to harm religion which alone triumphs,
  so there is no peace for them.

[Later in the poem]

We rely on God, the Omnipotent, the Mighty
  to help us, for He is Bountiful.
May He in His bounty preserve us from the trials
  and tribulations of the World,
And the Hereafter, and the day of Resurrection,
  when all rise up.
May we die in the Faith, go to Paradise,
  and see the Prophet.
May Aliyu be victorious for the sake of the Prophet
  who exceeds all mortals.

[Final verses]

The poem is ended, O God receive it
  for the sake of the Prophet;
May He pour blessings and peace upon him.
And upon His Companions, relatives, and
  all who followed him.
The date is 1259 [1843–44] from the time of the *Hijra*.[12]

Although the major period of Arabic writing in West Africa appears to be the sixteenth to the nineteenth century, there has, in fact, been more such writing in the twentieth century, even though European colonial occupation made English or French to be the official language of various different countries. But, nevertheless, some Muslim males pursued their education in Arab countries—especially in al-Azhar, the Islamic 'university' in Cairo.

Looking at more recent Arabic writing in West Africa: in Timbuktu Muḥammad Maḥmūd al-Arawānī (d. 1973) wrote a dozen items , plus some poems. One of the most interesting of his works was *Kitāb al-turjumān fī ta'rīkh al-Ṣaḥra' wa 'l-Sūdān* ['The Book of the Interpreter/ Translator on the History of the Sahara and Black Africa'], in 16 chapters, with one on the benefits of French rule.[13] Another scholar—one whom I once knew—was Aḥmad Bābēr al-Arawānī (d. 1997), an expert in matters of inheritance, an exegete, a *muḥaddith* [*ḥadīth* expert] , and a historian. One notable work was *al-Sa'āda al-abadiyya fī 'l-ta'rīf bi-'ulama' Tinbuktu al-bahiyya*['Endless welfare on knowledge of the scholars of the Splendid Timbuktu]—i.e. a history of Timbuktu and biographical dictionary of its scholars.[14] One interesting item, which he gave me some twenty years ago, was a list of the thirteen celebrated 'saints' of Timbuktu, together with a map of Timbuktu showing the locations of their graves .

A famous Nigerian scholar was Ādam 'Abd Allāh al-Ilūrī (d. 1992), a Yoruba man, originally from Ilorin. As early as 1952 he opened his first Arabic school in Abeokuta, and it was developed into the "The Arabic-Islamic Training Centre" (*Markaz al-Ta'līm al-'Arabī al-Islāmī*), which he re-established in Agege, a suburb of Lagos, in 1955. That center remained his physical and moral base for the rest of his life. The college graduated a large number of studentss, well trained in the Arabic language and the Islamic sciences, who have gone on to teach all over Yoruba territory. At -he also set up a printing press, which published many of his writings (a total of 76, including 6 poems), as well as other books and pamphlets that thereby became accessible to Nigerian Muslims.

Finally, here is information about how West African Arabic manuscripts have been preserved in the twentieth century, and what knowledge is now available about them, a matter that I have been concerned with. My first concern was in 1964 at the University of Ibadan (Nigeria), where I set up a "Centre of Arabic Documentation", getting manuscripts from the northern region of the country microfilmed and cataloged in an annual *Bulletin* of the Centre, together with articles on such topics. However, it is not clear that it continued to occur after I left that university at the end of 1966. However, in 1967 I was invited to a Unesco meeting of "Experts on Arabic Sources of African History", held in Timbuktu. At the end of the conference I signed up with many others on a recommendation to be sent to the government of Mali, asking them to set up a project for the conservation of Arabic manuscripts. So, in 1973, when the Mali government had obtained finance, mainly from Kuwait, they built in Timbuktu what was called the "Centre de Documentation et de Recherches Historiques Ahmed Baba [CEDRAB]", and got into it Arabic manuscripts, bought, or as gifts, from owners of manuscripts in the city, nowadays having a total of about 20,000 items. The original 9,000 manuscripts were later (1996–1998) catalogued in five volumes published in London (all in Arabic) by the Al-Furqan Islamic Heritage Foundation. That Foundation has also published catalogs of other Arabic manuscript collections in West Africa; one is a 3-volume catalog of a private collection in Timbuktu: the 6,000 items of the Mamma Haidara Library, run by Abdul-Kader [ʿAbd al-Qādir] Ḥaidara, with manuscripts inherited from his father, who died in 1980. Interestingly, Abdul-Kader is bringing some of his manuscripts to the United States in 2006 for an exhibition, to be held first at the International Museum of Muslim Cultures in Jackson, Mississipi, and then in the Du Sable Museum in Chicago in August 2006.

The Al-Furqān Islamic Heritage Foundation, based in London, has also published catalogs of Arabic manuscripts from Nigeria, Niger, and Senegal:

1. The Nigerian National Archives of Kaduna (1,645 items), edited and annotated by myself; 1 vol., 1997.
2. The University of Ibadan Library (422 items), also edited and annotated by myself; 1 vol., 2001.
3. Handlist of Manuscripts in the Libraries of Shaykh Serigne Mor Mbaye Cissé, al-Ḥājj Malick Sy & Shaykh Ibrāhīm Niasse, of Senegal (804 items), Compiled and edited by Ousmane Kane, 1 vol., 1997.
4. Catalogue of Islamic Manuscripts at the Institut des Recherches en Sciences Humaines, Niamey (2003 items), prepared by Hassane Moulay, 4 vols, 2005.

In Nigeria there are also public collections of Arabic manuscripts in Jos, Kaduna, Kano, Sokoto, and Maiduguri (Bornu). There are a also collections of West African manuscripts in the Africana Library of Northwestern University, Evanston [IL]:

1. The Umar Falke collection from Kano (3,500 mss.);
2. A collection of 400 various manuscipts. obtained in Nigeria by John Paden, the former director of the Program of African Studies at Northwestern University;
3. The John Hunwick collection—mainly 'published' manuscripts from northern Nigeria and from Senegal [i.e. handwritten works photocopied into paper-backed little 'books']—total 550 items.

The manuscript collection of the Africana Library also now contains copies of some 450 manuscripts photocopied from a collection of photocopied manuscripts in the African Studies Program of the University of Ghana, Legon (near Accra); a collection of the late Melville Haerskovits; and photocopies of some CEDRAB manuscripts.

Information on manuscript writings by West africans can be found in a published work that I have produced in two large volumes of *Arabic Literature of Africa*—including published (or translated) versions of them.[15]

Both volumes also include information on manuscripts in African languages other than Arabic: in Vol. 2: Hausa, Fulfulde, and Yoruba or Nupe; Vol. 4: Fulfulde, Hausa, Songhay, and Wolof. That is another aspect of "Arabic as the Latin of Africa" —when Muslims who could write Arabic, used the script to write their own languages, just as the English, and other Europeans, used the Latin script to write their own languages. In West Africa, the first such writing now known was in the mid-seventeenth century, when a man of the state of Kanem, just north of Lake Chad, wrote comments on the Koran in the local language of Kanuri, at the sides of a copy of the Koran in its original Arabic language.[16] In the next century (eighteenth) there was some use of the Arabic script to write the Fulani language [Fulfulde] in the Futa Jallon area of what is now Guinea; and it was also written similarly in northern Nigeria in the late eighteenth and the nineteenth century—most often for writing poems (e.g. Uthmān ɗan Fodio and his daughter Asmāʾu). In that same area, from the early nineteenth century, the local native language, Hausa, was written in the Arabic script—certainly in prose by Usmanu ɗan Fodio's brother, Abdullahi. In Nigeria the Nupe language was also written in Arabic in the nineteenth century, after the introduction of Islam in the middle region near the river Niger; also in the south, after the introduction of Islam and conversion to it by many Yoruba men, they also used the Arabic script to write their own Yoruba language. Two other West African peoples at least did a similar thing in the twentieth century: the Wolof of Senegal and the Songhay of Mali. In the latter it was mainly for writing poetry, and some manuscripts in Songhay still exist in Timbuktu.

Another volume on Arabic works in *Arabic Literature of Africa* will be Vol. 6: "Writings of the Western Sahara", to be prepared by me with Ulrich Rebstock and Charles Stewart, mainly covering Mauritania, where a great deal of Arabic writing has been done. I also hope to have a volume on West African languages in the Arabic script, at least for Fulani and Hausa in Nigeria and Cameroon, maily put together by two Nigerians who can deal well with such languages and scripts: Muhammd Sani Umar (on Hausa) and Hamidu Bobboyi (on Fulani).[17]

Chapter Seven

Non-Muslims and Muslims in the Arab World

(i) Non-Muslims

For many centuries the commonest way for West Africans to end up in the Arab world, especially in the Arab states in North Africa, was through slavery. Arabs were holding Africans as slaves in Arabia even before the beginning of the religion of Islam, though such Africans had come from the area of what is now Ethiopia. When Islam became the fundamental religion of Arabs, it became lawful only for people considered to be 'pagans' to be held by Arabs as slaves.

After taking over North Africa, some Arab/ Berber Muslims began trans-Saharan trade, obtaining some black Africans as slaves.[1] Not only were black Africans thought to be descendants of Ham through the curse of Noah, punishing Ham for observing his father's nakedness as he bathed, but it also came to be believed that, in accordance with the account in the Old Testament, or the Torah, the punishment made Ham and his descendants slaves of his brothers. In fact the Old Testament and the Torah do not say that Ham was turned black, but Arab thinking began to equate blackness with slavery. Another theorization of the nature of black people of Africa also charterized them as inferior beings based on a Greek view of the climatization of the known world and the relationship of climate to intelligence. This theory divided the world north of the equator into seven latitudinal zones, the ideal one being the fourth or middle zone, corresponding to the Mediterranean area, while the farther one got away from this zone (either north or south), the more extreme the climate became, and the less civilized its inhabitants were thought to be.

The notion that blackness of skin meant that a person was a slave continued to be assumed by many Moroccans down to the late nineteenth century. Evidence for this comes from the experience of a Muslim scholar, Muḥammad al-Sanūsī b. Ibrāhīm al-Jārimī, from the Timbuktu region who visited Morocco, apparently in the 1880s, and later wrote a small book in the mid-1890s (*Tanbīh ahl al-ṭughyān ʿalā ḥurriyyat al-sūdān*)[2] about his experience, and saying that he found there some uncivil Moroccans who claimed that all blacks (*sūdān*) were absolutely slaves, and that they did not deserve to be free; He then devoted the main part of his book to arguments against such a claim, arguing for the fundamentally free nature and human equality of black Africans, basing himself on sayings attributed to the Prophet, one of the most convincing of which is when Muḥammad said: "O people, your Lord is One, and your ancestor is one. The Arab has no virtue over the non-Arab, nor has the non-Arab over the Arab, nor has the White over the Black, or the Black over the White except in terms of devotion to God".

The conquest of North Africa soon brought about the conversion to Islam of a large proportion of the Berber populations of the region. It was perhaps this lack of a source for slaves, as well as information about the production of gold in western Africa, that then stimulated interest in establishing connections between the Arab conquerors and the populations of black Africa. In fact, before the end of the North African occupation, Arab military leaders had made a few explorations into the Sahara, through the Fezzan in the east, and over the Draʿ valley in the west. Both of these explorations were to become ways for the earliest trade routes, leading down in the east to the oasis of Kawār, from there to trade with the kingdom of Kanem to the north of Lake Chad; and in the west across the Sahara and the Adrar uplands to the town of Awdaghast, which had connections with the kingdom of Ancient Ghana.

Awdaghust was one of the early locations for the marketing of slaves. The Andalusian geographic writer Al-Bakrī recorded that the main population of Awdaghast (in the mid-eleventh century) was of North African Berbers, but he said there were also black women, who as good cooks were sold for 100 *mithqāls* each (i.e. roughly 42.5 grams of gold)[3] There were also light-skinned ("white") very attractive slave girls, the description of which implies they were used as concubines.[4]

In the following century, evidence of black slaves being taken across the Sahara to Morocco seems clear, since there were black soldiers serving the Almoravids,[5] a ruling group that originated from the southwestern Sahara, and had earlier taken control of Awdaghast, and such practice was continued by the Almohads in the following century.

Farther east, black slaves had been imported into North Africa even earlier. The first Aghlabid ruler of Ifrīqiya (basically what is now Tunisia), Ibrāhīm I (800–812), is said to have bought black slaves to relieve his subjects of forced labor and to provide his bodyguard with sword-bearers.[6]

These would no doubt have come across the Sahara from the Lake Chad region via a route passing through the Kawār oasis and the Fezzan to Tripoli, then part of Aghlabid territory, from where they could easily have been obtained by the Aghlabid ruler. Although the main objective of trans-Saharan trade was gold, slaves seem to have become the second most important item. The trade route south across the Sahara to the Lake Chad region must have had slaves as its principal trade objective,[7] since that particular trans-Saharan region was very remote from gold fields, which were then to the south of Ancient Ghana in an area between tributaries of the river Senegal, known as Bambuk. Later in the same century many more slaves were obtained by the Aghlabid ruler Ibrāhīm II (875–902), who made out of them a military force.[8]

By the fourteenth century there were evidently slaves being sent to North Africa from Hausaland, a trade no doubt conducted by Tuareg nomads. When Ibn Baṭṭūṭa was returning from West Africa to Morocco in 1353 he traveled from Takedda (just west of Aïr) to Tuwāt with a caravan containing six hundred female slaves.[9] They must have come from south of Takedda, and the clear connection would have been with Kano, or Katsina in northern Hausaland.

Farther east, the Nile valley was also a supply route for black slaves, to serve in Egypt, and later on in other areas of the Medi-terranean Muslim world. The passing of black slaves into Egypt from other areas of the Nile valley began in 652. However, when the Egyptian ruler Ibn Ṭūlūn (868–84) required slaves for military service, they probably did not come from south in the Nile valley, but across the Sahara from the Lake Chad region, through the Fezzan and via other east Libyan and Egyptian oases to Cairo. In the

10th century the next ruling regime in Egypt, the Ikhshīdids, also used large numbers of black slaves as troops, and when the Fāṭimids took over Egypt, ruling 969–1171, they also set up large battalions of black soldiers, no doubt obtained from West Africa, since the Fatimids came to take over Egypt after setting up their regime in Ifrīqiya, and subduing much of North Africa until the Almohads took it over.

In fact, every area of black Africa became a source of slaves for the Islamic world, proving to be the largest and most long-standing reservoir of slaves, continuing from central Sahelian regions (e.g. modern Republic of Chad) down to the beginning of the twentieth century. But some thousand years before that, some rulers of parts of the Sahelian region themselves converted to Islam, and their subjects soon began to follow them. This made such people unacceptable as slaves, but made it easier for Muslims from north of the Sahara to trade with them, and these new Muslim-ruled states themselves captured slaves from their non-Muslim neighbors, using some in trading relations, but also retaining some for their own use. Since Muslims could only enslave persons who were not Muslims at the time of capture, how would they make decisions about who were Muslims and who were not? This question later bothered purchasers of West African slaves in the Saharan oasis of Tuwat and in Morocco. In 1615 the Timbuktu scholar Aḥmad Bābā responded to such questions from persons in those two areas, who received slaves being exported from Timbuktu.[10]

In the late seventeenth century the ʿAlawī ruler [of Morocco] Mūlāy Ismāʿīl (*reg.* 1672–1727) decided to establish an army of black slaves, and even insisted on including in it all black men known as *ḥaraṭīn*, who were, in fact, free persons, some of whom had originally been slaves, but were by then free Muslims. Mūlāy Ismāʿīl argued that the *ḥarāṭīn* were simply slaves who had slipped the rope of servitude, which now ought to be reconnected, the assumption being that being black defined one as a slave. This attitude towards black Africans was still current in the nineteenth century when a West African Muslim scholar visited Morocco and found people claiming that "all blacks without exception were slaves, and not free people, for how should they deserve that being black of skin?"[11] At about the same time such a view was attacked by the Moroccan historian Aḥmad b. Khālid al-Nāṣirī, who argued that the people of Sudanic Africa were by and large Muslims, and hence could not be enslaved.[12]

Documents from eighteenth century Timbuktu provide evidence of the existence of slavery there too,[13] and no doubt this had also been the case in the sixteenth and seventeenth centuries, since Aḥmad Bābā's work shows that Timbuktu was a location of slave commerce, and some of the slaves brought there from distant areas would likely have been purchased by Timbuktu inhabitants.

The major topic of such documents is the freeing of slaves, a common feature of slavery in the Islamic world. To free a slave was a way to obtain divine forgiveness, in keeping with a saying of the Prophet: " If any man frees a Muslim slave, God will spare from Hell for every limb of the slave a limb of the liberator".[14] Thus, once a slave had converted to Islam (as most did), he or she stood a better chance of being freed, since only Muslim slaves were eligible for being freed. Some Muslims even saw slavery as a way of enlarging the world's Muslim community, since the road to freedom was through conversion to Islam. Freedom could be obtained in ways other than an immediate manumission, one of which was "post-mortem freedom" (*tadbīr*)", practised in Timbuktu, as evident from some of these documents. This way of ordering freedom of a slave following the owner's death could be granted to both males and females, but females also had another way of achieving this. If, as concubines, they bore a child from their master, they legally had guaranteed freedom upon the master's death, whilst the child was automatically free from birth, in keeping with paternalistic precedence; the father was free, therefore any child of his was free. This was how sons of concubines owned by askiyas could even become their successors.

Whilst Islamic law allowed a man a maximum of four formal wives, no limit was placed upon the number of slave women he could have as concubines. Even in North Africa, rulers sometimes owned black women as concubines, the most noteworthy of whom was the Saʿdian ruler of Morocco, ʿAbd al-Mālik (*reg.* 1576–1578), whose famous son, Sultan Aḥmad al-Manṣūr, the initiator of Moroccan conquest of the Songhay empire, was born by a Fulani concubine.[15] In Morocco in the late seventeenth century black slaves not only served as soldiers, but were formed into a special military force, known as the *ʿAbīd al-Bukhārī*, during the reign of *Mūlāy* Ismāʿīl al-Samīn (1672–1727), and, following the latter's death, they took control of political power, appointing and deposing seven of his sons between 1727 and 1757.[16]

It was recognized that moving a slave towards Islam was a duty of the slave's owner. It is probable that for slaves being taken across the Sahara to North Africa, an attempt would often be made to turn them into Muslims before they reached North African markets. Since most slaves taken to North Africa were used for domestic duties, and hence became part of a household, it would have been much preferable for such a slave to be a Muslim rather than a"pagan". Muslims would not wish to have pagans as part of their household. In the nineteenth century, a slave caravan coming from Katsina stopped at somewhere near Aïr, where there was an Islamic "hermitage"(*zāwiya*). Just before they left, one of the members of the *zāwiya* said to them: "O Muslims! These negroes you are bringing are idolaters. We must make them know the One God; we must teach them to pray and how to perform ablutions; we must circumcise them today. God will reward you for it. Make your slaves assemble. By God's grace we know their language; we will put ourselves in the middle of them and teach them what it is good for them to know".[17]

However, even if African slaves converted to Islam, they did not always totally abandon some of their previous beliefs and practices. A non-Islamic cult, practised by some of the Hausa, survived among slaves taken over to Tunisia. An account of this religious cult, known as *bori*, is provided by a Fulani scholar and son of a *qāḍī* from Timbuktu, Aḥmad b. Abī Bakr b. Yūsuf, who was returning from pilgrimage in 1813, and stayed for a while in Tunis. He portrayed *bori* as a women's cult centered round a female idol, who seemed to stand at the head of various other idols whom the slave women worshipped and made sacrifices for, especially to cure sickness. The patient, in his words, "prostrates to their gods, and if the one in charge of the ceremony is a slave woman who commands the *jinn*, the patient prostrates to the jinns, who are in her head.[18] Then they say to him, 'Your requests are granted', and they order him to make slaughter to their gods every year on the same day. Every year they take from him what he has, and he may grow poor by this means".[19] Such practices continued long after this Timbuktu scholar's account, *bori* being investigated in both Tunis and Tripoli, a century later, by a British anthropologist.[20]

Enslaved black Africans, taken up to North Africa were not only kept there, but some were sold and transferred across the Mediterranean Sea. Some were sent over to the area that is now Turkey; that being the home of the Ottoman Empire that dominated the Islamic world from the late thirteenth century. Many of such male slaves—sent there from the late sixteenth century—were turned into eunuchs, so they could serve the sultans by looking after their harems containing slave mistresses.

In North Africa many West African slaves were eventually freed. In Algeria, by the mid-nineteenth century, there were still some eighteen thousand slaves in areas controlled by the French, but also some three thousand who had been freed.

Hence, many West Africans ended up as citizens of North African states, even more when, in the twentieth century, French rule in them did not permit slavery.

(ii) Muslims

Even though, to some extent, Arabs often thought that black human beings must be slaves, West African Muslims clearly demonstrated their religious faith, especially when making pilgrimage to Mecca; so they were respected, and none considered to be slaves, since it was truly forbidden to enslave a Muslim.

Mansa Mūsā, the ninth ruler of the empire of Mali, from 1312 to 1327, was a devout Muslim, and decided to make the pilgrimage to Mecca in 1324. Leaving from his capital close to the river Niger he went north to Walāta and across the Sahara to the oasis of Touat, accompanied by a large number of soldiers and with some five hundred slaves, each of whom is said to have carried in their hands items of gold weighing over four pounds each, some of which were given away to nomadic tribes of the Sahara. He then moved on to Cairo, and speaking Arabic well, he was much appreciated by the Sultan of Egypt Nāṣir al-Dīn, who favored him, as reported by the famous traveller Ibn Baṭṭūṭa:

> He sent a rich present to [the Mamlūk sultan] al-Nāṣir. It is said that it included 50,000 dinars. Al-Nāṣir accomodated him at al-Qarāfa al-Kubrā and gave it to him as a fief. The sultan received him in his audience room, talked to him and gave him a gift and supplied him with provisions. He gave him horses and camels, and sent along with him emirs to serve him until he performed his religious duty in the year 1324.[21]

Then he passed on to Arabia, visiting the tomb of the Prophet Muḥammad in Medina, and performing his pilgrimage ceremony in Mecca. There he met with an Andalusian poet and juristic scholar, Abū Isḥāq Ibrāhīm al-Sāḥilī from Granada, and agreed with him to accompany him back to Mali.

Back in Cairo after his pilgrimage, he had honors bestowed upon him again by the Mamlūk sultan, who was generous in his gifts. It is said that

Mansa Mūsā had prepared in his country for his expenses a hundred loads of gold, each weighing three qintars [totalling about 300 lbs]. This was all exhausted, and he could not meet his expenses. He therefore borrowed money from the principal merchants; and, he sold to them the palace which the sultan had bestowed on him as a gift.

On his way back to Mali in 1325, Mansa Mūsā stopped in Timbuktu, which had been occupied by the Mali Empire with much else of the Middle Niger area in the 1290s.

While staying there he arranged the construction of the "Great Mosque"—*Jingere Ber*—at the south-western corner of the city, which still exists as a beautiful Islamic house of worship.

After his return to his Mali capital, he permitted Abū Isḥāq Ibrāhīm al-Sāḥilī to stay in Timbuktu and later make a visit to Morocco around 1337, where he was well received by the Marīnid sultan Abū 'l-Ḥasan. There he wrote a poem encouraging the sultan to attack the Zayyānid ruler of Tlemcen and occupy that area, which he did, and then the ruler of Mali sent an embassy to Fez to congratulate the Marīnid sultan. Hence cordial relations were promoted between the rulers of Morocco and Mali, and the Marīnid sultan reciprocated Mansa Mūsā's courtesy through a high-ranking ambassador of his own, accompanied by magnificent gifts. Diplomatic relations between Mali and Morocco continued for several decades.

Another celebrated West African ruler who performed the pilgrimage and spent some time in Egypt was the founder of the Askiya dynasty as ruler of the Songhay Empire, Askiya Muḥammad b. Abī Bakr. He left his capital of Gao in late 1496, accompanied by 1,500 soldiers, taking with him 300,000 mithqāls, obtained from his predecessor Sunni ʿAlī.[22]

In the next year he got to Mecca and performed pilgrimage cerecmonies, then going for a brief stay in Cairo. There he met the famous author Jalāl al-Dīn al-Suyūṭī, who had an interest in the Muslims of West Africa; and several of his huge number of writings have been studied in West Africa—especially in Timbuktu. Askiya Muḥammad spent some time studying with al-Suyūṭī, who also wrote for him a small work on government drawn from *ḥadīth* literature: *Al-Aḥādīth al-mutqana fī faḍl al-salṭana.*[23]

Also, according to the Moroccan historian Muḥammad al-Ṣaghīr b. ʿAbd Allāh al-Ifrānī:

> In Egypt he met the ʿAbbāsid caliph and asked him to authorize him to rule the sub-Saharan area of [West] Africa (*bilād*

> *al-sūdān*), and to be vice-gerent (*khalīfa*) for him there. The ʿAbbāsid caliph delegated to him authority over the affairs of those regions, and made him his lieutenant over the Muslims [who dwelt] beyond him. The pilgrim [Askiya Muḥammad] returned to his land and based his leadership on the principles of the *sharīʿa* and acted in accordance with the way of the people of the Sunna.[24]

Hence Askiya Muḥammad became a 'caliph' of the caliph of the Islamic world, entitled to be in charge of all of the Muslim lands of West Africa (*al-Takrūr*), though he did not take over any area outside of what had become, under the ruler before him, Sunni ʿAlī, the Songhay Empire.

After him, four sons, and then three grandsons, took on rule of Songhay and inherited his 'caliph' position.

Some other Muslim rulers of West Africa performed pilgrimage, but none gained such a status. Many Muslim scholars also went to Mecca, often spending some time in Egypt during their return home. For example:

> [Aḥmad b. ʿUmar b. Muḥammad Aqīt] in the year 1485.. travelled to the east and perfomed pilgrimage, coming into contact with Jalāl al-Dīn al-Suyūṭī, Shaykh Khālid al-Waddād al-Azharī, the 'imam' of grammar, and others. He returned during the time of upheaval caused by the tyrant Sunni ʿAlī, and went to Kano and other cities of the land of the Blacks (*bilād al-sūdān*). Many people benefitted from his teaching of the Islamic sciences, the most illustrious of them being the jurist Maḥmūd b. ʿUmar, who read the *Mudawwana* with him. He exerted himself to gain knowledge of the Islamic sciences and to teach them right down to his death, which occurred on a Friday night in Rabīʿ II, 946 [17 Sept.–15 Oct. 1536], at about the age of eighty.[25]

On another Songhay scholar Muḥammad b. Aḥmad b. Abī Muḥmmad al-Tāzakhtī:

> He travelled to the east in the company of our master, the jurist (*qaḍī*) Maḥmūd [b. Aḥmad b. ʿAbd al-Raḥmān], and came into contact with illustrious scholars such as the *Shaykh al-Islām* Zakariyya [al-Anṣārī] and the two Burhāns—al-Qalqashandī and

> Ibn Abī Sharīf—and ʿAbd al-Ḥaqq al-Sunbāṭī and others. With them he studied the Science of *Ḥadīth*, both auditing and relating Traditions. ...In Mecca he was granted licences by Abū 'l-Barakāt al-Nuwayrī, by ʿAlī b. Nāṣir al-Ḥijāzī, by Abū 'l-Ṭayyib al-Bustī, and others. Then he returned to land of the Blacks (*bilād al-sūdān)* and settled in Katsina, where the ruler showed him favor and appointed him *qāḍī* of the city.[26]

So West African Muslim scholars going into the Arab world gained more learning of Islamic topics, and then expanded this to others in West Africa.

The West African who learned most and altered his beliefs, and then influenced other Muslims, was Ṣāliḥ al-Fullānī, a man from the Futa Jallon in Guinée, who spent much of his life in Medina from 1775. With great study of the 'sayings of the Prophet Muḥammad' (*ḥadīth*), he became convinced that it was religiously most justifiable to learn and interpret *ḥadīth*s rather than just following up on what Islamic law-schools (*madhāhib*) had promoted. Keen on this anti-*madh'hab* attitude, he taught his views to others in Medina, including one or two scholars from India; and later, after their return to India an anti-*madh'hab* movement was established, known as the *Ahl al-Ḥadīth*. It was also in India that his writing on the topic, *Īqāẓ himam Ūlī 'l-abṣār* was published in A.H. 1328/1910–11.[27]

Some other West African Muslim scholars–especially Senegalese–have spent time the Arab World, notably in Cairo, studying at the Al-Azhar university–an institution that was set up over a thousand years ago, and in the past century has had contacts with West Africa and encouraged Muslims to study there. Occaisionally some senior scholars of Al-Azhar themselves went to cities in West Africa and inspired local Muslim scholars.

(iii) Arabs in West Africa

Not only did West African Muslims go into the Arab world, but some Arab Muslims—mainly from North Africa—made visits to West Africa. The full information on some, who probably went across the Sahara to do trading, is not known, but evidently they were to provide information to Arab geographers, who then included information about West Africa in their writings. One of the earliest, and most celebrated, was Abū ʿUbayd al-Bakrī of Andalusia, who wrote in the eleventh century.[28] He lived in Andalusia, but got information from Andalusian and Maghribī merchants, who had travelled across the Sahara—through what is now Mauritania—and were able to provide knowledge of Ancient Ghana between R. Senegal and R. Niger, which came in his book *Kitāb al-masālik wa 'l-mamālik.*[29]

In the next century another man, probably born in Morocco, wrote geography with areas of West Africa; Abū ʿAbd Allāh Muḥammad al-Idrīsī.[30]He wrote on much of the Sahel, from the zone of Takrūr, just north of the river Senegal, over the Middle Niger, including Gao (*Kawkaw*), and as far east as Kānem, west and north of Lake Chad.

Arabs, whose travels into West Africa are known about, are the following:

(i) Ibn Baṭṭūṭa, a fourteenth century man, whose home was in [what is now] Morocco, and made some thirty years of travel in the world: in the Middle East, several times in Mecca; in eastern Europe; in Asia–even in China; in eastern Africa; and after his return to Morocco, the ruler asked him to go to West Africa, so he did so in 1352–3; he went over to Walata (*Īwālātan*) and then found his way to the city of the ruler [capital] of the Mali Empire on the River Niger.[31] There he stayed for six months, having contact with the ruler Mansā Sulaymān, and afterwards travelled to the Middle Niger, visiting Timbuktu, where Abū Isḥāq al-Sāḥilī, the Andalusia poet, was staying. Ibn Baṭṭūṭa then moved on to Gao and next to Takedda–location of a copper mine–to the north of Aïr, and then returned to Morocco, passing through the oasis of Touat.[32] His return journey took place accompanying a caravan taking six hundred female slaves over to Morocco.[33]

Another important North African who visited West Africa in the 1490s was Muḥammad b. ʿAbd al-Karīm al-Maghīlī (b. *c.* 1440), whose origin was in Tlemcen, and first spent time in the Touat oasis, having the synagogue in Tamantit destroyed, some Jews killed, and the rest diverging to other oases.[34] From there he went across the Sahara, doing some teaching in Takedda, and then going on to Kano, the sultan of which, Muḥammad Rumfa, he had corresponded with, he spent several years in Kano, becoming the father of three sons. For the sultan he wrote a 'treatise of advice".[35] He then moved on and spent a brief time in Katsina, and then moved on to Gao, where he collaborated with Askiya *al-Ḥājj* Muḥammad, providing responses to seven issues that were making problems for the ruler of Songhay.[36]

Shortly after that time, the Songhay Empire and other Sahelian areas were visited by a traveler from Morocco. He was born in Fez, named al-Ḥasan b. Muḥammad al-Wazzān al-Zayyātī, whose parents had moved over from Andalusia; and, on return from pilgrimage by boat in 1518, he was captured by Italians, who presented him to Pope Leo X, and a year later the pope baptized him and gave him his own personal name; and being 'African', he was then known as Leo Africanus, and it was in Rome that he soon wrote in Italian an account of his many travels, published in Venice in 1550.

Leo Africanus did much travel in North Africa, and in the early sixteenth century went through much of the Sahel region of West Africa, going through Walata, and along the river Niger from Jenne through Timbuktu and Gao, and then eastwards to Gobir and Agades, and southwards to Katsina, Kano, Zegzeg (Zaria), and to Bornu. In his book he put useful information on the areas he visited,[37] but did not have any political interrelations with them.

These were not the only North African Arabs who crossed over to an area of West Africa. One notable interconnection was of men from Ghadames—a city in western Libya;[38] many of them, engaged in merchant practice, went over to Timbuktu in the late sixteenth century and became residents in the southern zone of Timbuktu—to the east of the Jingere-Ber mosque. Others also went to Kano and to Katsina, staying long in those cities.

Chapter Eight

Arab Views of Black Africans and Slavery

Black Africans were the earliest type of slave known to Arabs, and were the latest imported into the Arab-Islamic Middle East. One of the very first black Africans known to have been in slavery in the Arabian peninsula, and to have become one of the first to have converted to Islam, was the Abyssinian called Bilāl [b. Rabaḥ], who was owned and then freed by Abū Bakr, the Prophet Muḥammad's father-in-law and later successor (caliph), to whom he gave his freed slave, who then accepted the Prophet's message and was given the position of muezzin—"caller to prayer" by Muḥammad. Soon afterwards, North Africa was occupied by Arab Muslim armies in the late seventh century, black Africans were traded over the Sahara, and bought by Arab merchants as slaves—a practice which continued down to the early twentieth century.

However, Arabs had no grounds for assuming that all black people were justifiably to be seen as slaves. The only enslaveable persons were those defeated in battle against Muslims.The basis of this may be gathered from what the Qur'ān said to the Prophet Muḥammad in defining what women it was lawful for him to live with: "We have made lawful unto thee... .those whom thy right hand possesseth of those whom Allah hath given thee as spoils of war".[1] So it was captives in battle who might be "owned"—in this case females, but later applied to both females and males. Since war could not be fought against other Muslims, only "unbelievers" (*kuffār*) could be captured and held onto as slaves, and no consideration was ever given in Islamic teachings to what color of skin made people enslaveable unbelievers. While the Qur'ān recognizes that human beings are of many different types: "We established you as peoples and clans, so you may know one another", it then defines the most honored as the most devout, i.e. no ethnic group is automatically favored by Allāh.[2] Commenting on this, the Prophet Muḥammad said; ""White has no preference over black, nor black over white, except through devoutness".[3] On another occasion the Prophet is said to have said: "The Arab has no virtue over the non-Arab, nor has the non-Arab over the Arab, nor has the White over the Black, or the Black over the White except in terms of devotion to God. Surely, the noblest of you in God's sight is the most devout."[4]

Such teachings, however, did not fully influence Arab minds over their views of black Africans. The first century and a half of Islam, as the Arabs went forth from the Arabian peninsula to conquer half of the known world, was marked by an overwhelming sense of Arab superiority over all other peoples. In this period even to become a Muslim one had to become a sort of fictive Arab by being adopted as the client of an Arab tribe.[5] The conquered peoples as a whole were in fact referred to as the 'clients' *(mawālī)*, and Islam was viewed as the property of the Arabs. This, in turn, produced a reaction among the conquered peoples who rose to defend themselves and declare their equality with Arabs, using the adopted Arabic language to express themselves, and often adopting heterodox forms of Islam as the symbol of their opposition to Arab dominion. This had varying results. In the central lands of the Middle East population speakers of languages such as Coptic in Egypt, Syriac and Aramaic in Syria and Palestine. and Chaldean in Iraq, adopted Arabic as their language of learning and of daily speech and, by and large, adopted Arab manners, customs and ways of thinking. Farther east the Iranians defiantly stuck to their ancient tongue, in daily speech and much of their literature, and created a distinctly Iranian Islamic culture. In the West the Berbers of North Africa either became arabised or, if they clung to their indigenous language and culture, became largely marginalised.

Equality of the believers, then, could have different practical expressions. What, then, did it mean for black Africans? On this I will begin with a quotation from the writings of Bernard Lewis, one of the few contemporary scholars to deal with issues of race and color in Islam:

> While the exponents of religion preached a doctrine of equality, albeit in somewhat ambiguous terms, the facts of life determined otherwise. Prevailing attitudes were shaped not by preachers and relaters of tradition but by the conquerors and slave owners who formed the ruling group in Islamic society. The resulting attitude of contempt—towards non-Arabs in general, and toward the dark-skinned in particular—is expressed in a thousand ways in the documents, literature, and art that have come down to us from the Islamic Middle Ages..... This literature and, especially, popular literature depicts [the black man] in the form of hostile stereotypes—as a demon in fairy tales, as a savage in stories of travel and adventure, or commonly as a lazy, stupid, evil-smelling and lecherous slave. The evidence of literature is confirmed by art. In Arab, Persian and Turkish paintings blacks frequently appear, sometimes as mythological figures of evil, sometimes as primitives or performing some other menial task, or as eunuchs in the palace or in the household. Yet in spite of these attitudes and the resulting disabilities imposed upon men of African birth, they nevertheless managed to make a significant contribution to mediaeval Islamic civilization—and not only in their labor and services.[6]

Beginning with the last point Professor Lewis makes, i.e. the contribution made by men of African birth to medieval Islamic civilisation, let us examine the extent to which prejudice against them may have restricted their opportunities for making such contributions. Arabs had black Africans living among them from before the days of Islam—mainly, it would appear as slaves. Some of the African women bore children from Arab fathers, but the males among them seem to have had some trouble being accepted as full members of the tribe, despite the weight given to patrilineal descent. The sons of African mothers and Arab fathers, as well as slaves who had been given their freedom, were, or became, thoroughly arabised in language and culture and sought to participate with 'pure-bred' Arabs on an equal footing. They were often to find, however, that their skin color stood in the way. Some took up the art of poetry, the quintessential Arab medium of artistic expression, and these black poets form the subject of a fascinating book by the Egyptian scholar ʿAbduh Badawī called [in translation] "The Black Poets and their Distinctive Characteristics in Arabic Poetry" (*al-Shuʿarāʾ al-sūd wa-khaṣāʾiṣuhum fī 'l-shiʿr al-ʿarabī*).

These poets were often known as 'the ravens of the Arabs' (*aghribat al-ʿarab)* because of their black color, and as one satirist pointed out, ravens were traditionally considered bad omens, and were especially associated with the parting of lovers. On the relationship of their color to their social status and to their poetic art, Badawī has this to say:

> [T]here was a sharp sensitivity over color among the black poets before Islam. This was because they were a depressed and downtrodden group and because they were excluded, sometimes roughly, sometimes gently, from entering the social fabric of the tribe. Thus they lived on the edge of society as a poor and depressed group. They were only acknowledged under conditions of extreme pressure, as we know from the life of [the poet] ʿAntara. Although this poet was the defender of his tribe and its supreme poetical voice, his own tribe's attitude towards him continued to pain him and weigh on his mind. The name 'son of a black woman' stuck to him, even when returning from victory in battle.
>
> Although the tone of uneasiness becomes softened among the poets of the time of the Prophet as a result of Islam's raising the morale of the black man, yet the sensitivity over color is not altogether different. The poets saw themselves and their people as downtrodden and although this sense of being downtrodden varied from century to century and from poet to poet, yet the black man could not refrain from being a voice of protest against the life around him and the tragedy of his own situation. Later we see [black poets] exploding in the face of those who allude to their color as may be seen in the poetry of the 'three angry poets' al-Ḥayquṭān, Sunayḥ & ʿAkīm [of the early eighth century]. For them it was not enough just to defend themselves. We see them taking pride in their blackness and in the history of black people and the lands they came from and attacking the Arabs on the points on which they prided themselves.[7]

Here ia an example of this. One of these poets, who was insulted in some obscene verses by the Arab poet Jarīr, responded in the following way:

> Though I be frizzle-haired, coal-black of skin,
> My generosity and honor shine yet brighter.
> Blackness of skin does me no harm
> When in battle's heat my sword is flailing.
> Would you claim glory where there is none?
> The Ethiopians are more glorious than you.[8]

As contacts with sub-Saharan Africa expanded, Arabs in the broadest sense simply labeled such populations as *sūdān*, i.e. "blacks", though peoples from some regions of Africa who were taken into the Middle East in slavery were given broad ethnic labels such as the Zanj from East Africa or the Ḥabasha/ Abyssinians from the Horn of Africa. Eventually some Arab writers made attempts to draw up an ethnography, relating "peoples" they had encountered to some scheme of humanity they were familiar with, initially grounded in what they viewed as religious authority. Wahb b. Munabbih, a south Arabian of part-Persian origin (d. 728), who was considered an expert on Jewish legends (*isrā'īliyyāt*), is credited with the following statement:

> Ham, the son of Noah was a white man, fair of face. God—Mighty and Exalted is He—changed his color and the colors of his descendants, because of the curse of his father. He went off, and his offspring followed him, and they settled on the sea shore. God increased and multiplied them, and they are the Blacks (*al-sūdān*).[9]

Not only were black Africans thought to be descendants of Ham through the curse of Noah, who punished Ham for observing his father's nakedness as he bathed, but it also came to be believed that, in accordance with the account in the Old Testament or the Torah, the punishment made Ham and his descendants slaves of his brothers Shem and Japheth and their descendants, i.e. Arabs, Europeans, and central Asians. In fact, the Old Testament and the Torah do not say Ham was turned black, but Arab thinking began to equate blackness with slavery.

Another theorization of the nature of black people of Africa also charterized them as inferior beings based on a Greek view of the climatization of the known world and the relationship of climate to intelligence. This theory divided the world north of the equator into seven latitudinal zones, the ideal one being the fourth, or middle, zone, corresponding to the Mediterranean area, while the farther one got away from this zone, the more extreme the climate became, and the less civilized its inhabitants.

The great fourteenth century historian Ibn Khaldun did not find acceptable the theory of blackness being related to descent from Ham, and denied the soundness of the claim, as follows:

> Some genealogists who had no knowledge of the true nature of beings imagined that the Blacks are the descendants of Ham, the son of Noah, and that they were characterized by black color as a result of a curse put upon him by his father (Noah), which manifested itself in Ham's color and the slavery that God inflicted upon his descendants. Concerning this they have transmitted an account arising from the legends of the storytellers. The curse of Noah upon his son is there in the Torah. No reference is made there to blackness. His curse was simply that Ham's descendants should be the slaves of his brothers' descendants.[10] To attribute the blackness of Negroes to Ham, shows disregard for the nature of heat and cold and the influence they exert upon the air and upon the creatures that come into being in it.[11]

On the other hand, Ibn Khaldūn fully accepted the theoretical division of the then known world into seven zones. He also basically accepted that this system had built into it a hierarchy of value judgements about the inhabitants of the various areas of the world, though he grappled with how most "scientifically" this could be explained.

Mediterranocentric theory had long taught that extreme heat in zone 1 and extreme cold in zone 7 produced distorted and savage human beings. As one got farther away from these regions, so climates became more moderate and people more civilized. It is not difficult to see where this led to. As already observed, the fourth zone, which was right in the middle of the seven, and hence the most moderate in its climate and the most civilized in its inhabitants, was the Mediterranean zone.

This view of the world can be illustrated by two quotations from earlier authors. The first is a Persian geographer of the early tenth century [Ibn al-Faqīh al-Hamadhānī] who quotes someone whom he merely describes as "a man of discernment" in regard to Iraqis:

> The people of Iraq have sound minds, commendable passions, balanced natures, and high proficiency in every art, together with well-proportioned limbs, well-compounded humors, and a pale brown color, which is the most apt and proper color. They have been well baked in wombs that do not expel them [prematurely] with a blondish or reddish color, with grey-blue eyes and whitish eyebrows, such as occurs to the wombs of the Slav women or those like them or comparable to them. The wombs of their women do not overcook them until they are burnt, so that the child comes out something black or pitch-black, malodorous and pungent-smelling, with peppercorn hair, unbalanced limbs, a deficient mind, and depraved passions, such as the Zanj, the Ethiopians, and other blacks who resemble them. The Iraqis are neither unbaked dough nor one cooked and burnt, but between the two.[12]

Europeans, then, are seen as unbaked (or half-baked), and Africans as burnt; but while the author seems to hold only the Europeans' color against them, his description of Africans reveals prejudices which go beyond color and are formulated by racial stereotypes. Descriptions such as 'malodorous...... with unbalanced limbs, a deficient mind and depraved passions' include indictments of moral character, but they are not uncommon in writers of the medieval period. A fourteenth century Syrian writer, the geographer Al-Dimashqī (d. 1327), who draws copiously on earlier writers and adds little which is original, echoes some of these prejudices:

> The equatorial region is inhabited by communities of Blacks who are to be numbered among the savages and beasts. Their complexions and hair are burnt and they are physically and morally deviant. Their brains almost boil from the sun's excessive heat...... The human being who dwells there is a crude fellow, with a very black complexion, burnt hair, unruly, with stinking sweat, and an abnormal constitution, most closely resembling in his moral qualities a savage, or animals. He cannot dwell in the second zone, let alone the third and fourth, just as

> the people of the first zone live not in the sixth, nor those of the sixth in the first, or the equatorial region, because of the difference in the quality of the air and the heat of the sun. God knows best![13]

Later he expands upon this:

> We shall now give an account of what has been said about the inhabitants of the seven zones in regard to their physique and their moral qualities, and the reasons for this. The first zone is from the equator, extending to what lies beyond it and behind it. It contains the following nations: the Zanj, the Sūdān, the Ḥabasha, the Nūba, etc. Their blackness is due to the sun . . . Since its heat is extreme and it rises over them and is directly over their headswice in a year, and remains close to them, it gives them a burning heat, and their hair, pursuant to the natural processes, becomes jet-black, curly and peppercorn-like, closely resembling hair that has been brought close to a fire until it has become scorched. The most convincing proof that it is scorched is that it does not grow any longer. Their skins are hairless and smooth, since the sun cleans the filth from their bodies and draws it out. Their brains have little humidity for similar reasons and hence their intelligence is dim, their thoughts are not sustained, and their minds are inflexible, so that opposites, such a good faith and deceit, honesty and treachery, do not coexist among them. No divinely revealed laws have been found among them, nor has any divine messenger been sent among them, for they are incapable of handling opposites together, whereas divine laws consist of commanding and forbidding, and creating desire and fear. The moral characteristics found in their belief systems are close to the instincts found naturally in animals, which require no learning to bring them out of the realm of potentiality into that of reality, like the braveness to be found in a lion, and the cunning in a fox.[14]

In an attempt to grapple with some of these stereotypes and explain them in a more scientific fashion, Ibn Khaldūn had this to say:

> We have seen that Negroes are in general characterized by levity, excitability, and great emotionalism. They are found to dance wherever they hear a melody. They are everywhere described as stupid. . . . . Al-Masʿūdī[15] undertook to investigate the reason [for this]. However, he did no better than to report on the authority of . . . al-Kindī[16] and Jālinūs[17] that the reason is a weakness of their brains which results in a weakness of their influence they exert upon the air and upon the creatures that come into being in it.[18]

He goes on to explain that heat expands the "animal spirit" (i.e. the emotional side of human nature), and gives the example of the merry drunkard whose animal spirit is heated by wine and the man who breaks into song when immersed in a hot bath. Hence it is to be expected that people who live in hot climates will be merrier than those who live in colder climes, and to make his point he contrasts the "cheerful" Egyptians with the "gloomy" Moroccans. So, though he endorsed the stereotype of the light-hearted, light-footed, emotional black African, he sought to deny that such characteristics are due to inherent mental inferiority and to give these alleged racial characteristcs what he considered a "scientific" explanation related to climate.

We have come some way from theories about Slavs being undercooked in the womb and black Africans being overdone, but these 'scientific' explanations for color or other characteristics do not alter the fact that, in medieval Arab eyes, extreme whiteness and extreme darkness of skin were considered aberrations from the norm and were to be connected with extremes of climate. These extremes, in turn, were thought responsible for other departures from the "golden mean", which was, by definition, what prevailed in the Mediterranean lands.

For all his inquiring mind and his attempt to apply scientific and materialistic principles to the explanation of human behaviour and social organization, Ibn Khaldūn still could not escape from the clutches of the ancient theory of the division of the world into seven climatic zones, and in fact sought to use this as a basis for what he thought was a scientific explanation for the alleged characteristics of different peoples. But this was, in reality, nothing more than a new way in which to rationalize stereotypes and to make prejudices respectable. In his celebrated *Muqaddima,* or "Prolegomena" to his universal history, he gives an explanation for what he (and no doubt the majority of his Arab contemporaries) considered to be the barbarous characteristics of the black Africans of the first zone and their reflection in northern Europeans of the seventh:

> The inhabitants of the zones that are far from temperate, such as the first, second, sixth and seventh, are also farther removed from being temperate in all their conditions. Their buildings are of clay and reeds, their foodstuffs are sorghum (*durra*) and herbs. Their clothing is the leaves of trees that they sew together to cover themselves, or animal skins. Most of them go naked. The fruits and seasonings of their countries are strange and inclined to be intemperate. In their business dealings they do not use the two noble metals [silver and gold], but copper, iron, or skins, upon which they set a value for the purpose of business dealings. Their qualities of character, moreover, are close to those of dumb animals. It has even been reported that the Negroes of the first zone dwell in caves and thickets, eat herbs, live in savage isolation, a do not congregate, and eat each other. The same applies to the Slavs[i.e. northern Europeans in general] . The reason for this is that their remoteness from being temperate produces in them a disposition and character similar to those of dumb animals, and they become correspondingly remote from humanity.[19]

From this we might understand that Nigerians and Norwegians, or Ghanaians and Germans share parallel traits. He then contrasts the charcteristics of the people of these outer zones with those of the middle zone—the Mediterranean lands—and the two zones adjacent to them:

> The inhabitants of the middle zones are temperate [i.e. well-balanced] in their physiques and character and in their ways of life. They have all the natural conditions necessary for a civilized life, such as ways of making a living, dwellings, crafts, sciences, political leadership, and royal authority. Thus they have [the various manifestations of] prophecy, religious groups, dynasties, religious laws, sciences, countries, cities, buildings, horticulture, splendid crafts, and everything else that is well balanced.[20]

This passage is remarkably self-congratulatory and, by implication, very dismissive of the peoples whose lands lie outside the middle zones. However, its strict application created paradoxes that forced Ibn Khaldūn into some re-thinking and the formulation of a rider to his theory. For him there were two problems. First, Ibn Khaldūn knew from both personal experience and historical investigation that his theory about the barbarism of black Africa and its peoples simply did not hold water. He had gathered a great deal of information about the kingdom of Mali, and had met men who had had close contacts with the great ruler of Mali, Mansa Mūsā during his early fourteenth century pilgrimage. He had also met other West Africans in various places in North Africa, including emissaries of rulers, and could not comfortably dismiss them and their countries as barbarous. Secondly, it must have been something of an embarrassment to have to admit that the Arabian peninsula, the home of the Arabs and the cradle of Islam, lay partly in the first zone and partly in the second zone—regions that were supposed to be, by reason of their harsh climates, zones of barbarism whose people were remote from civilisation and humanity.

What new theories could he propound to deal with such contradictions? In regard to the Arabian peninsula he produced a climate modification theory under which it was argued that because the Arabian Peninsula was surrounded by water on three sides, this reduced the dryness of its air and hence the intemperance of character that the dry heat would otherwise cause. As we have seen, a combination of heat and dryness in the air was thought to dessicate brains and produce perverted temperaments.

His explanation for the evident fact that the peoples of Sahelian West Africa (the only ones he had direct knowledge of) were civilized people with kingdoms, dynasties, crafts etc.—in short all those attributes that made for a balanced, 'temperate' way of life—relies on a completely different type of argument. Indeed, the whole theory of the effect of climate on human character and culture was thrown overboard in favor of an argument based on religion. Following the passage quoted earlier on the barbarity of the inhabitants of tropical Africa and northern Europe, he further castigates these peoples for being "ignorant of prophecy" and lacking in a religious law, meanng they are not Muslims nor do they belong to a religion recognized by Muslims as being of divine inspiration, such as Christianity or Judaism. For al-Dimashqī the very barbarism of such peoples, induced by climatic factors, was the reason why they had not been favored with prophecy. Ibn Khaldūn, however, does not view their barbarism as irredeemable; on the contracy, they may escape it through the adoption of a revealed religion. Hence he could then make exceptions to the rule of barbarism for denizens of the climatically extreme zones who had adopted Christianity, such as the Ethiopians and certain peoples of Europe, or those who had become Muslims, such as the people of most of the Sahelian region of West Africa (i.e.Mali, Senegal, and the Middle Niger area). In short, faith was to be the touchstone of civilized humanity and, as far as West Africa was concerned, what served to exclude some of its peoples from their otherwise "natural" categorization as barbarians was, in the eyes of Ibn Khalđun, their profession of the faith of Islam.[21]

The bond of the brotherhood of the faith not only meant that a black man/woman who was a Muslim ought no longer to be regarded as a barbarian, but that he or she should no longer be regarded as an inferior in any way when compared to an Arab.

There was, however, a different approach to one group of black Africans, who were not, in the main, Muslims. that is the people known as Ḥabasha—a name no doubt semantically related to the English term "Abyssinia [Habashinia]. Although medieval Arab writers might sometimes use the term simply as an equivalent of the term *sūdān* (i.e. black Africa), its primary focus was on the area we now call "Ethiopia". A considerable literature was produced on the virtues of Ethiopians, even though many slaves originating from that area were owned in the Arab world (particularly in Arabia and Egypt). The reason for this is no doubt that Ethiopia was a refuge for Muslims who were persecuted during the Prophet's lifetime, and the king of Ethiopia at that time was thought by some to have embraced Islam. The Prophet Muhammad glorified him by naming him as one of the three blacks, or Ethiopians, who were, in his words "masters (*sādāt*) of Paradise", one of the others being his adopted freed slave and first muezzin[22] of Islam, Bilāl.

The titles of a number of writings in the medieval period express the superiority of black (or at least "dark-skinned") people over whites (or "light-skinned") people. One of the earliest was by a famous Iraqi writer of the ninth century, al-Jāḥiẓ, whose short treatise was called "The Glory of Blacks over the Whites" (*Fakhr al-Sūdān ʿalā 'l-bīḍān*). In the twelfth century another Iraqi writer, Ibn al-Jawzī, wrote a book with the translated title "Illumination of darkness concerning the merits of the Sūdān and the Ethiopians". In the fifteenth century, a celebrated Egyptian writer, al-Suyūṭī, wrote a book called "Raising the status of the Ethiopians" (*Rafʿ shaʾn al-ḥubshān*). Another work of his deals with preferences for skin color—light, dark and brown, forming an anthology of verse in praise and satire of women of different skin colors. This clearly indicates that color was an issue in the medieval Arab world, but some of the poetry emphasises the admiration for black women, as may be seen from these poetic quotations :

> Pearl is the name of many a black girl
> How amazing it is to have a black pearl!
> Night of union with a black woman is shiny bright
> How amazing to have a night that is white.[23]

Thus, although black Africa was largely a "region of the mind" creating negative images of black people, personal contact, especially with women as concubines, could produce love and appreciation. Another poet, in love with a black woman called Tuktum, humorously praises her color, comparing it implicitly to the blackness of musk and of darkness:

> I love black women for Tuktum's sake.
> For her sake I love all who are black.
> Show me anything with scent that's as sweet as musk,
> Or better for resting than after dusk.[24]

In fact, attitudes towards black women were generally more positive than they were towards black men, even if the women were of slave origin. More female slaves were taken across the Sahara to North Africa than men, and such women were then retained as concubines by Arab men. Some were even made mothers of children for rulers. In such cases the children born were considered free, since their fathers were free, and patrilineality was the social norm in Arab society. In one case such a child, a male, became a successor to his ruling father—Sultan Aḥmad al-Manṣūr, whose mother was a Fulani concubine, and he ruled Morocco 1578–1608.

Such tolerance for wholly black persons, even when technically "free" was not so common in Morocco. In fact, the notion that to be black meant to be a slave became a commonly held belief. Sultan Aḥmad al-Manṣūr began to set up a black slave military force for his kingdom after the conquest of the Songhay empire and the exportation to Morocco of men considered to be slaves. About a century later *Mūlāy* Ismāʿīl b. al-Sharīf decided to do a similar thing, and initiated such a force by searching for descendants of those who had been part of the earlier slave army. The search, however, collected anyone viewed as a "black" throughout certain areas of Morocco.

This included some who were said to be *ḥarāṭīn*, that is free blacks, who had lived in Saharan oases, being perhaps original inhabitants of such areas, but many of whom later migrated into Moroccan locations including some cities—not least of which was Fez. Objections from scholars of Fez were rejected by Mūlāy Ismāʿīl, who argued that he had proven that such persons (or their ancestors) had originally been slaves, but had deserted their owners and scattered themselves around the country. Such an argument clearly bases itself on the assumption that to be black is to be a slave. Finally several thousand blacks were collected together and trained as soldiers forming a group known as *ʿAbīd al-Bukhārī*, and then black women were seized and the ruler arranged marriages between these women and the armed blacks so as to eventually produce later generations of black "slave origin" men to continue serving in a military force.

The notion that blackness of skin meant that a person was a slave continued to be assumed by many Moroccans down to the late nineteenth century. Evidence for this comes from the experience of a Muslim scholar [Muḥammad al-Sanūsī b. Ibrāhīm al-Jārimī] apparently from the Timbuktu region, who visited Morocco apparently in the 1880s, and later wrote a small book [*Tanbīh ahl al-ṭughyān ʿalā ḥurriyyat al-sūdān*] about his experience, and said at the beginning:

> I found there some uncivil Moroccans who claimed that all blacks (*sūdān*) were absolutely slaves, and that they did not deserve to be free; how would they deserve that being black-skinned?" . He then devoted the main part of his book to arguments against such a claim, arguing for the fundamentally free nature and human equality of black Africans, basing himself on sayings attributed to the Prophet, one of the most convincing of which is when the Prophet said: "O people, your Lord is One, and your ancestor is one. The Arab has no virtue over the non-Arab, nor has the non-Arab over the Arab, nor has the White over the Black, or the Black over the White, except in terms of devotion to God.

The equivalence of blackness of skin with slavery continues to be reflected in the Arabic dialects spoken by many Arabs; i.e. *ʿabīd* = blacks. In 1995 in Nigeria, when I was speaking in Arabic with a Lebanese, he simply referred to Nigerians as *ʿabīd*, and a modern dictionary of Egyptian spoken Arabic also defines *ʿabd* first as 'slave', and secondly as 'negro'.[25]

The association of black Africans with slavery, then, has been in the Arab mind from the lifetime of the Prophet Muḥammad until the present, although Muḥammad himself did not promote such a concept, but rather denied it. The first black Africans known to Arabs in Arabia were Ethiopians taken into tribes as slaves. Then, as Arab-ruled territory expanded to include northern Africa, the first major source of slaves was black Africa, which also remained a major source of slaves down to the dawn of the twentieth century when European colonial rule took over. Although Islamic teachings defined the enslaveable merely as "unbelievers", no matter of what color, non-Muslim black Africans were evidently easier to get hold of and bring into the Arab regions of the Muslim world, especially after populations of the Sahelian region became Muslims and could use captured non-Muslim neighbors as trading objects for commerce with the Mediterranean world. For many centuries a false interpretation of the Torah account of Ham's son Canaan becoming a servant of his brothers, made Ham himself both a slave and a man who was turned black through his father Noah. Later, an allegedly "scientific" theory claimed that inhabitants of black Africa, due to the extreme heat of their climate, were weak-minded "savages". All of these theories tended to make Arabs see black Africans as inferior human beings whom they could claim as slaves.

Finally, here is what may be found in the Qur'ān about human colors:

> 3 (*Āl ʿImrān*), 106: "On a day some faces will be whitened and some blackened. As for those whose faces are blackened (it will be said) 'Did you reject Faith after your belief of it?' Then taste the penalty for rejecting Faith."
>
> 30(*S ūrat al-Rūm*):22: "Among His signs is the creation of the heavens and the earth, and the differences in your languages and colors".

The commentator Al-Bayḍāwī' says:" Whiteness of skin and blackness of it, or the layout of limbs and their shapes and colors, and their quality, so that there occurs distinction and recognition until there is difference in dual harmonizing together with conformity of their materials and the matters encountered by the two of them in smoothing [massaging?] ".

Although these quotations seem to condemn black Africans, it is quite evident that many black Africans who converted to Islam have been true worshippers of God and acting in respect of all orders of the Qurʿān.

Chapter Nine

African-Arab Relations in the Twentieth Century[1]

At the dawn of the twentieth century the entire African continent, with the exception of Liberia, Ethiopia, Morocco and Libya, was in the grip of European colonialism. Libya, which was suffering the dying throes of Ottoman Turkish imperialism was soon to exchange this servitude for that of a European power too—the Italians, who took control of it in 1912, while Morocco had 'protectorate' status forced on it by the French in 1911. New economic and political orientations rapidly came about. Territories were sharply delineated by fixed boundaries put in place by the imperial powers, and movement between territories was discouraged. In particular, the British and the French endeavoured to minimise the contacts which their Muslim subjects in West Africa could have with the Muslim lands of North Africa and the Middle East, through careful control of the right to travel, including the right to travel to Mecca for pilgrimage, and through surveillance of their subjects who had betaken themselves to cities such as Cairo. In the economic sphere the introduction of cash crops in West Africa and the payment of taxes in cash gave European trading companies a privileged position and directed the flow of trade towards the coast. In northern Africa the French territories of the Maghrib were rapidly re-oriented towards France—a process which had begun in Algeria as early as the 1830s—while Egypt continued a flirtation with Europe which had begun in 1798 when Napoleon forced his attentions upon that country, and which was pursued thereafter by successive Egyptian rulers, from Muḥammad ʿAlī onwards.

These economic and political re-orientations which came about in part, from what we may call 'natural' factors inherent in European control of African territories, were further and deliberately reinforced by factors more artificially created. The introduction of European education, largely placed in the hands of missionary organisations, served to introduce and then reinforce very specific views about a benevolent Christianity and a benevolent Europe while at the same time denigrating Islam and Arabs. These latter two terms were often used as synonyms. and great emphasis was placed on what was called—often without much accuracy—the 'Arab' slave trade and 'Arab' rapacity, greed and cruelty. The existence of a slave trade between West Africa and the Arab lands, involving both Muslim Arabs and Muslim West Africans is a fact of history, as was amply delt with in Chapter 2 above.. But the European missionaries and educators who stressed this did so with the aim of alienating their converts and potential converts against Islam and in the interests of a colonial divide-and-rule policy. In this they were most successful, since the slavery issue remains to this day the major psychological barrier dividing Arabs and (non-Muslim) Africans, though it must be said that Arabs have often helped to maintain it by denying the existence of the slave trade or grossly underplaying its importance. Needless to say, what suffered most in this ideological battle was indigenous African religion and customs. If the Christian missionaries and the Muslims could agree on one thing, it was that they were both superior to 'heathendom' and its 'idols' and 'false gods'. The stage was thus set for a battle between these two religious 'superpowers' which is still being played out in several African countries today with disastrous consequences for national unity and development.

There were two great thinkers and apostles of pan-Africanism who, in very different ways, helped to bridge this gap which European imperialism wanted to widen between Africans south of the Sahara and Arab Africans to the north of it and between Christians and Muslims in Africa in whichever geographical zone they lived. The elder of the two, Edward Wilmot Blyden was born on the Caribbean island of St Thomas in 1832 and, after being denied admission to a college in the United States because of segregationist laws, settled in Liberia, completed his studies there and went on to become a professor, a statesman and a diplomat, dying in 1912. Though a product of a Christian upbringing and, indeed, trained by the Presbyterians, he became increasingly well disposed towards Islam, and in 1869 went to Cairo to study Arabic. In his book *Christianity, Islam and the Negro Race* (published in 1887) he openly promoted Islam as a progressive and civilizing force which was well able to be of moral and material service to Africa. Indeed, he essentially made that argument which later became part of the teachings of the Black Muslim movement in America and which can still be heard in some quarters today that Islam is the 'natural' religion of Africa and of people of African descent, though he did not express it precisely in those terms.[2] By the same token, though himself a practising Christian, he was still critical of the methods of European missionaries in Africa, pointing out that it was used by them to create a sense of servility in Africans. Although Blyden believed that a period of tutelage to Europe (such as he saw Africa undergoing in his day) was necessary and inevitable, he firmly believed that this was a temporary state and that Africans must continually prepare themselves through education and self-awareness to take their rightful place in what he perhaps naively believed would be a non-racist world.

The younger, but as yet less well-known of the two, was in many ways the mirror image of Blyden. Duse Mohamed Ali was born in Egypt in 1866 of mixed Egyptian and Sudanese parentage. He was thus, biologically, a perfect Afro-Arab, though intellectually he was as much a European as an Arab or an African, since he spent his formative years in school and college in England. Though a successful actor and playwright in England in the 1890s and 1900s, from the beginning of the second decade of the twentieth century he increasingly turned his energies to historical and political writing and to political activism. In 1911, the same year as the publication of his friend Casely-Hayford's *Ethiopia Unbound,* Duse Mohamed brought out his book *In the Land of the Pharaohs,* a history of modern Egypt viewed from a strongly nationalist and anti-imperialist viewpoint. In the following year he and Casely-Hayford together with a group of other West African intellectuals in London founded *The African Times and Orient Review* inspired by the First Universal Races Congress, that had just been held in London and at which, among others, W. E. B. DuBois had read a paper. The journal aimed to create a forum for the ideas, aspirations, and grievances, of African, Arab and Asian peoples dominated by imperialism, and its contributors over the eight years of its life included such influencial figures as Herbert Macauley, Joseph Casely-Hayford, Marcus Garvey (who worked on the journal in 1913) and Booker T. Washington.

In 1931, after many years of writing and lecturing, including several lecture tours in the United States, Duse Mohamed settled in Nigeria where he spent the remaining 14 years of his life as a journalist, nationalist activist and promoter of liberal Islamic views among the Lagos Muslim community. Not the least of his achievements were the founding of the weekly (later twice weekly) *Comet*, which had an important influence on nationalist thinkers in Nigeria and, in its strong condemnation of the Italian invasion of Ethiopia in 1935, served to create pan-Africa awareness; and in the year before his death his election to chair the historic meeting of trade unionists, political activists and students out of which was born the first pan-Nigerian political party, the NCNC.

These two African intellectuals who tried, by both the pen and by living example, to form some sort of bridge between Arab and non-Arab Africa and between Muslims and non-Muslims regrettably had few imitators, nor yet were there many clear opportunities before the 1950s for Arab and non-Arab Africans to deliberate upon the commonalities that might exist between them. There were anti-colonialist gatherings such as the 1927 Conference of the Oppressed Peoples held in Brussels and attended by such figures as Nehru, Ho Chi Minh, George Padmore and Masali al-Hadj and various student organisations in European capitals (notably Paris and London), which served to foster nationalist and anti-imperialist sentiments, but there was relatively little sign that the two halves of Africa saw themselves as very closely linked or potentially sharing a common destiny. The one occasion on which Arab-African solidarity seems to have been manifested was in the Ethiopian crisis of 1935 when Egyptian nationalists were the first to form a solidarity committee and to recruit Egyptian officers to serve with the Ethiopian army.

Perhaps all this is not very surprising. During the inter-war years much of the energy which went into the emerging movement of Pan-Africanism came from African-Americans or African Caribbeans such as Marcus Garvey and W.E.B. DuBois, whose agendas were closely linked to the problems of Africans of the New World diaspora. Hence the term Pan-African for them had more to do with the advancement of black Africans and their descendants as a group than it had with any notion of the solidarity of all peoples of the African continent. There seems, in fact, to have been few possible points of contact for black Africans and Arab Africans who suffered under the colonial yoke. West Africans from British ruled territories in West Africa sought their higher education in London or, in a number of notable cases such as those of Nnamdi Azikiwe and Kwame Nkrumah, in the United States. The language problem, if nothing else, ensured that Arab Africans would not seek educational opportunities in such places. West Africans from French-ruled territories of course went to Paris and there, at least in theory, it would have been possible for them to have met with Algerians or other North Africans from French-ruled territories. But apart from the Communist-inspired Union Intercoloniale in the early 1920s in which Algerians such as Mesali Hadj and Hadjali Abdelkader met with West Africans such as Louis Hunkarin and Tovalou-Houenou (and in which Ho Chi Minh played a leading role), there seems to have been little contact or solidarity between colonial subjects from north and south of the Sahara. Egypt, which became nominally independent in 1922, had a number of institutions of higher education of its own which were amalgamated into a national university in 1925. Those who were sent abroad for training were sent to France. Perhaps influenced by Kemal Attaturk's attempts to modernise Turkey by europeanising it, as well as by their own European experiences, Egyptian intellectuals of this period tended to see their country more as an extension of Europe than as a part of Africa. Their contacts with black Africans apart possibly from a few Sudanese who shared their language and Islamic culture—certainly seem to have been minimal. Immediately following the Second World War in 1945 Egypt became a founder member of the Arab League (together with Iraq, Syria, Lebanon and Jordan) and for some years its interest in regional groupings was confined to this one.

In 1952 came the revolution which was to shake the Arab world to its foundations and which was to have a profound effect on movements for freedom from colonial domination; indeed, it was to show colonised peoples throughout the world that the imperial masters could be defied and ultimately compelled to retreat from the territories they controlled. Although the coup by the Free Officers headed by Colonels Neguib and Nasser, was primarily aimed at overthrowing the corrupt monarchy of Egypt, it rapidly took on a much wider role as champion of those who struggled for independence in Africa and the Arab world. Egypt's position was, and is, a very special one in the African-Arab world for a number of reasons both geographical and historical. First of all, it sits in a strategic position at the junction of the Asian and African Arab worlds and at the physical cross-roads of the two continents. It has been the gateway through which African Muslims, whether Arab or non-Arab have had to pass on their way to Mecca for the annual pilgrimage. It has also had an Islamic university, al-Azhar, for over a thousand years and this has been a point of attraction for African Muslims seeking higher education. Secondly, it has long-standing historical links with the lands of the Nile valley to its south through what is now the Republic of the Sudan from Pharaonic times down to the nineteenth century when it directly ruled the Sudan for some 60 years. Its complete dependence on the river Nile for its food production means that an important segment of Egyptian foreign policy will always be concerned with the lands through which the Blue and White Niles flow—Sudan, Ethiopia and Uganda. Thirdly, in the context of the 1950s, its eastern borders were blocked by the existence of the state of Israel which inhibited direct contact with the Arab countries of Asia except by air. Egypt, of course, did not think in terms of Israel, but rather in terms of occupied Palestine. Egypt had fought in the 1948 war against the new state and, indeed, Nasser had taken part, emerging from it disgusted at the corruption in high places which had been responsible for supplies of outdated weapons, deficient ammunition and irregular supplies of food and medicine. The experience, in fact, further strengthened his resolve to reform Egypt and rid it of the monarchy—a process which ended up in the July revolution. Finally, it must be remembered that Egypt had for centuries been ruled—and in great measure misruled—by foreigners and non-Arabs for centuries: the central Asian and Circassian Mamluks from 1250 to 1517, the Ottoman Turks from 1517 to 1798, the French, then the independent Ottoman dynasty of Muḥammad ʿAlī (a Macedonian by birth) which was itself subjected to British overrule from 1882 to 1922. King Fārūq himself, whom Nasser overthrew and exiled, was the last and perhaps the most despised of this line. This, then, is the background against which we must see Nasser's virulent anti-imperialist stance and his clear and genuine concern for African liberation.

Nasser understood well Egypt's situation in relation to the Arab world, the African world and the wider Islamic world, and he knew that history had forged for Egypt an intricate relation with all three which he could ignore only at his, and Egypt's, peril. He explained all this in his brief book *The Philosophy of the Revolution*, published in 1954, the year in which he ousted General Neguib and assumed undisputed leadership of the revolution. The key passage on Egypt's relationship to the rest of the African continent reads as follows:

> [We] cannot under any condition, even if we wanted to, stand aloof from the terrible and terrifying battle now raging in the heart of that continent between five million whites and two

> hundred million Africans. We cannot stand aloof for one important and obvious reason —we ourselves are in Africa.
>
> Surely the people of Africa will continue to look at us—we who are the guardians of the continent's northern gate—we who constitute the connecting link between the continent and the outer world. We certainly cannot, under any conditions, relinquish our responsibility to help spread the light of civilisation and knowledge up to the very depth of the virgin jungles of the continent.
>
> There still remains one more reason—the beloved Sudan, whose boundaries extend to the heart of the continent where it is bound by neighbourly relations, being the sensitive centre.[3]

Despite the somewhat patronising terms in which this message is couched, with seeming overtones of 'the white man's burden' and the 'civilising mission' of Egypt, it is quite clear that c saw Egypt as involved with, and committed to, the struggle against European imperialism in Africa and it is possible to read his clumsy phrase 'the light of knowledge and civilisation' as a harbinger of the technical aid and scholarships for higher education which Egypt liberally offered to many African countries in the 1960s. His reference to 'the beloved Sudan' is a little more ambiguous. He certainly hoped that as Sudan moved towards independence (which it achieved in 1956) it would vote to gain this in a union with Egypt, which remained nominally a partner in the Anglo-Egyptian Condominium and this would seem to underlie his specific mention of the country here. However, when the Sudanese voted for total independence Nasser accepted this with good grace, though in pursuit of Egypt's Nile valley interests he did explore the possibilities of a tripartite union with Sudan and Ethiopia in 1957 but it came to nothing.

Nasser's first opportunity to put his revolutionary views on public display came in 1955 with the Bandung conference of non-aligned nations which was also attended by representatives of Ethiopia, Libya, Liberia, Sudan and the Gold Coast among African nations. It was here that he took on the self-imposed role of spokesman for the African nationalist movements and champion of the rights of the Palestinians and accuser of Israel. On the first issue Egypt continued to play a useful and important role, while the second issue proved to be an Achilles Heel in Arab-African relations, as will be seen in what follows. Egypt also organised and held in Cairo an

Afro-Asian Solidarity Conference in December 1957, as if to show that Egypt was the logical locus for such Third World anti-imperialist gatherings after Bandung. But before Nasser's policies for the liberation of Africa could be put into effect he had to face a severe threat to his rule and, indeed, to the independence of Egypt. The withdrawal of British troops from the Suez Canal Zone, the nationalisation of the Canal and the ensuing tripartite aggression of France, Britain and Israel fully occupied Nasser's energies in 1956, but by the time it was over and the invading powers had been compelled to go home with their tails between their legs, Nasser had emerged in the eyes of the Third World as a hero of resistance to imperialism, a symbol of a developing nation that could stand up to major European powers and win the day. He had further demonstrated Egypt's independent and non-aligned status by concluding a deal on arms with Czechoslovakia, thus breaking the monopoly in this field hitherto held by western countries and bringing down their anathema upon him.

It was now that Nasser made a bid for leadership of Africa by giving his support to any and every anti-colonialist movement on the continent (sometimes more than one in a single country), allowing them to open bureaux in Cairo and providing their representatives with generous salaries and travel privileges. Uganda was the first to open a bureau in 1957, followed by Kenya in 1958, and the ANC in 1960. At various times movements as diverse as the Algerian FLN, FRELIMO, the PAIGC, the MPLA, SWAPO and ZANU all had bureaux there. Egypt's radio transmitters were also busy in the late 1950s and in the 1960s, broadcasting up to 8.5 hours a day to Africa, not only in Arabic, English and French, but also in Swahili, Lingala, Somali, Amharic, Shona, Hausa and Fulfulde.

Here, then, was an entry on a grand scale onto the stage of African and Afro-Arab politics, but it did not go unchallenged. Immediately upon Ghana's independence in 1957 Dr Kwame Nkrumah began actively to pursue a leadership role in fostering unity among African peoples and fighting colonialism in Africa. In rapid succession he called a Conference of Independent African States in Accra in April 1958, forged a union with Guinea (which had just said the 'historic no' to France) in November 1958 and in the following month convened at Accra the All African Peoples Congress. In the same year he also sanctioned the establishment of diplomatic relations with Israel, much to Egypt's discomfort, and accepted a $20m loan from Israel. Later, in 1960, Israel concluded an agreement with Ghana to create and train a Ghana Air Force and to create a Flying School.

This marked the beginning of a tug-of-war between Ghana and Egypt for the leadership role in independent Africa's affairs and in the support of African liberation movements. It also signalled the beginning in earnest of a tug-of-war between Egypt and Israel for influence in independent Africa, a struggle in which, on the Arab side, Algeria and much later Libya and Saudi Arabia eventually took part, but each for its own ends with little unity of purpose (indeed, sometimes rivalry) between them. Israel, not surprisingly, was also conducting its African policy for its own ends as part of its broader fight for world recognition and influence and specifically to break out of its encirclement by hostile Arab countries by gaining influence on countries that lay to their south or west. It was especially anxious to refurbish its image as a struggling developing nation which the Tripartite Aggression of 1956 had turned into one of a collaborator with imperialism. On the material side it had a broad array of aid packages to offer (essentially underwritten by American aid) ranging from scholarships and training schemes in Israel to loans and military aid and advice. On what may be called the moral side, it offered the image of a new nation which had 'made the desert bloom' in its ten years of independence—an inspiration for new African nations—and a view of Jews and Africans as sharing a common legacy of suffering at the hands of Europeans. This latter sense of solidarity did not, however, stop Israel from maintaining strong commercial links with South Africa and collaborating with the apartheid state in matters of military technology and later nuclear secrets, as it still does to this day. The years 1960–64 saw a flurry of Israeli activity in Africa. Newly independent states sent high-level delegations to Israel while Prime Minister Golda Meier visited some ten African countries including Guinea, Ivory Coast and Ghana. As part of Israel's strategy to 'contain' the Arabs, special effort was put into improving relations and providing military aid to countries bordering the Nile valley, notably Ethiopia and Uganda. Through these two countries military aid could be passed to southern Sudanese fighting the Khartoum government, thus maintaining a destabilised Sudan which would in turn be in no position to support Egypt militarily in any confrontation with Israel. Later in the 1960s Israel was to give covert support to seccessionist Biafra, partly for cynical reasons and to offset Egyptian help to the Federal side, but also because the legacy of the Holocaust gave Israelis a natural sensitivity to Biafran claims of genocide.

In these and in so many other ways sub-Saharan Africa began to get itself embroiled willy-nilly in the issue which was of consuming interest to all Arabs in the 1960s and 1970s—the Palestinian question. Egypt in particular, but all other Arab countries to a greater or lesser extent, used whatever diplomatic weapons were available to them to persuade non-Arab African countries to break relations with Israel and in some cases and for certain periods of time (notably after the 1967 Arab-Israel war when the occupation of Sinai could be represented as occupation of part of an African country) they were successful. On the other hand Israel has fought with great skill and persuasiveness to maintain or renew its relations with African countries and to counter Arab influence south of the Sahara. African countries have sometimes been the winners in this contest for influence by accepting offers from both sides, but on balance the rivalry has no doubt had negative effects since it has perverted the course of development and has certainly steered the countries of Arab and non-Arab Africa farther and farther away from the ideals of African unity, and from greater inter-regional co-operation which might otherwise have been developed.

If Egypt was the main player from the Arab side in relations between West Africa and the Arab world in the 1950s and 1960s, the death of Nasser, the oil crisis of the 1970s and the de-radicalisation of Egypt under Sadat certainly changed this. The entry of Libya into both inter-Arab and inter-African politics after Col. Muammar Ghadhafi's coup in 1969 also put a new face on things. The oil crisis which increased the oil importing bill of non-producing African coutries some nine-fold between 1973 and 1975 was a severe blow to African-Arab co-operation and understanding. African countries, many of whom had broken ties with Israel before 1973 or did so soon after the October War in solidarity with Egypt, praised the Arab countries' use of the 'oil weapon' after the war to punish Israel's backers and in partcular the United States. But there was to be a sting in the tail on the one side and some harsh recriminations on the other. Immediately following the 1973 Arab-Israeli war came the OPEC price hike, and although OPEC is more than merely an Arab organisation (and, indeed, includes two West African countries), the Arab countries that stood to gain most from the price hike were singled out for opprobrium by black African countries. In November 1973 a small Oil Emergency Fund was started up by the six Arab members of OPEC for the benefit of non-Arab, non-oil producing coutries. But its capital of $200m to provide loans maturing in 8 years was considered derisory. African countries,that felt they had showed their solidarity with the Arab world over the Palestine question by cutting their ties with Israel, thus forfeiting Israeli aid and technical assistance, wanted a preferential price for oil, and this the Arab countries refused, fearing that it might be abused and that, through it, oil might reach countries it had boycotted. An editorial in the *Zambian Daily Mail* at that time summed up what a lot of Africans thought (even if they did not say it) and again showed how Arab-African relations continued to be bedevilled by the ghosts of the past:

> Refusal by Arab countries to sell oil to Africa countries at a reduced price is a tacit (*sic*) example that Arabs, our former slave masters, are not prepared to abandon the rider and horse partnership. We have not forgotten that they used to abuse us like herds of cattle and sell us as slaves.[4]

The upshot was that later the OAU[5] was allowed to decide the criteria for the disbursement of the fund, which was doubled, while interest was cut to 1% and repayment set at 25 years with a 10 year grace period. As a result, between 1974 and 1977 over $221m was loaned to African countries, including major loans to Ethiopia and Tanzania and to Sahelian countries hit by drought. Arab countries also contributed to the OPEC Special Fund to aid developing countries hit by the oil crisis, providing some 40%, or $600m, of its funds. Arab aid for Africa also came on a bilateral basis through development funds set up by Kuwait (from 1961), Abu Dhabi (from 1971) and Saudi Arabia (from 1974), the latter fund disbursing 45% of its aid to African countries. The most effective source of Arab aid for Africa has come from a specialised organisation set up in 1973, the Arab Bank for Development in Africa. It was established with the express purpose of financing development in non-Arab African countries and to provide technical assistance for development. Aimed at the poorest and least developed countries it makes low-cost loans, typically at 4.5% with a repayment period of 20 years and a grace period of 5 years on average.

All of these various schemes have had their critics in non-Arab Africa. The major criticism is exactly the same one which is also directed against aid from Western countries, to wit, that it is in the form of loans which have to be paid back—perhaps when exhange rates have become much less favourable to the borrowing country—and that the loans are mainly directed towards financing imports—including *oil*—and to supporting balance of payments deficits. They also argue that what is needed is an increase in trade in terms of overall volume between the two regions and an improvement in the balance of trade from a general situation in which Arab countries export to sub-Saharan African countries twice as much as they import from them. African countries have not been slow to voice their criticisms while on the other hand—to quote the Sudanese expert on Arab-African relations, Professor Mohamed Omer Beshir:

> Arab countries became aware that arguments such as 'we are brothers', 'we are not colonizers' and 'we are not exploiters' are not convincing to Africans, that the alliance [between Arabs and Africans] was vulnerable, not only because of inherent weaknesses in both their economies, but also because of the international system in which they [both] operate.[6]

Before dconcluding this study, there are two other factors in contemporary Arab-African relations that I would like to consider. The first is the Gadhafi factor and the second is the factor of Islamic resurgence. It is now over thirtty years since Col. Muammar Gadhafi overthrew an effete monarchy. King Idris, although he belonged to the great Sanūsī family-cum-religious brotherhood which had led resistance to the French in Chad in the 1890s and to the Italians in Libya in the 1920s and 1930s, was regarded as a British stooge and Gadhafi's coup was considered by many to herald another revolution similar to the one initiated in Egypt in 1952. Gadhafi certainly saw himself as a second Nasser, whom he greatly admired, and whose mantle he felt had fallen upon him after Nasser's death in 1970. However, Gadhafi neither learned from Nasser's failures nor did he benefit from his successes. Nasser's 1958 union of Egypt and Syria to form the United Arab Republic had been beset with difficulties and had been dissolved after only five years. This did not prevent Gadhafi from attempting to initiate unions with Egypt and the Sudan (1969), with Egypt and Syria (1971), with Egypt alone (1972), with Algeria (1973), with Tunisia (1974), with Chad (1981) and with Morocco—this latter union surviving, at least on paper, from 1984 to 1986. None of these proposed unions was thought through carefully and none was ever more than symbolic. Gadhafi's political naiveté and mercurial character were sufficient to discourage other heads of state from too close an embrace. Whereas Nasser showed his revolutionary spirit by fostering and supporting anti-colonial movements of liberation in Africa, Gadhafi's contribution has been to support what he considers to be radical opposition groups *within* independent African countries aimed at toppling regimes which he adjudges reactionary, or supporting regimes no matter their ideology or human rights reputation—such as Amin's in Uganda or Bokassa's in the Central African Republic (and briefly Empire)—if they would support him or the causes he championed.

This policy was tried in a dozen African countries in the 1970s and 1980s, most egregiously in Chad, where Libya supported various factions between 1970 and 1986 and eventually got itself militarily involved to its great cost in terms of men, supplies and prestige. The lesson of Nasser's disastrous military intervention in the Yemen between 1963 and 1966 was evidently lost on Gadhafi. His creation of an Islamic Legion, to which were recuited young Muslim men from many African countries, bandying about of the word *jihād* and suggestions that Christianity should be expelled from Africa, also served to create deep suspicions in many quarters in sub-Saharan Africa. His policies towards the Sudan have been contradictory. First he supported Nimeiri against an internal coup in 1971, then supported coups against him in 1975, 1976 and 1983. Before Nimeiri's downfall he gave support to the Sudanese Peoples Liberation Army; soon he was reported to be helping the government of Gen. Bashir against the SPLA with Libyan planes and pilots.[7] All this has served to portray him in African eyes as an unpredictable meddler in the affairs of other countries. Thus it was that in the early 1980s many African countries broke diplomatic relations with Libya and in 1982 Col. Gadhafi was effectively denied the opportunity to serve as Chairman of the OAU. In all of this it has been clear that he has been acting on behalf of no one but himself and that his African policies in no way represent broader Arab policies, but popular stereotyping does not always make these necessary distinctions. In fact, it is salutary to bear in mind that, except at the level of multi-country donor bodies such as the Arab Bank for African Development, each Arab country has its own policy towards each African country on a bilateral basis and that there is no collective 'Arab policy' towards black Africa. Not only that, but we should remember that Arab countries have often been deeply divided among themselves, their greatest display of unity (or near unity) being over the boycotting of Egypt following the Camp David Peace Accords.

Perhaps where there is most suspicion and tension in relations between sub-Saharan African countries and the Arab world is precisely at the level of that organisation which should bring them closest together—the OAU. The problem here is that no less than eight of the members of the OAU are 'Arab' countries (if we include the ambivalent Sudan in that classification) and these eight countries (plus Somalia which seems to have been considered an 'honorary' Arab country) are members of the OAU by virtue of their being physically located on the African continent since geographical location is the primary qualification for membership in that body. On the other hand,membership of the Arab League is more exclusive and is based upon culture and language—the major anomaly being Somalia. By definition, no African country which does not have such a profile can belong. Thus many sub-Saharan Africans see that the Arab countries of Africa have the double advantage of belonging to both organisations and may at times be torn by dual loyalties. They also feel that what are 'purely Arab problems'—such as the Palestine problem—are foisted upon African countries who do not need them. Such anxieties, even, one might say, such fears, become the more intense in the perceptions of non-Muslim Africans who are ever conscious of what they see as the 'weight of Islam', represented most clearly by the Arab world, bearing down upon them from the north. No doubt the creation of the Afro-Arab Standing Commission which was the principal achievement of the First Afro-Arab Summit Conference held in Cairo in 1977 has done much to allay such feelings, but the ghosts of the past take long to be laid.

Mention of 'the weight of Islam', however, brings me to a discussion of the last of the major factors influencing African-Arab relations. Although the Islamic factor was the subject of an entire lecture of minr, I would like to make a few further remarks, especially about the way in which Islamic activism is affecting some African countries and how this in turn affects African-Arab relations. Despite the existence of important Christian minorities in several Arab countries—in particular Lebanon, Syria and Egypt—Islamic religion and culture are inseparable from Arab identity. Arabs, even including many very secularised intellectuals, are proud of the role Islam has played in shaping Arab culture and in the legacy of Arab culture which the adoption of Islam has brought to so many peoples. That 'light of civilisation and knowledge' which Nasser spoke of may also be read at a certain level as code for Islam and Arabo-Islamic culture. African Muslims also often subscribe to such views and look at Arabness as the ultimate cultural expression of their faith. Fluency in the Arabic language, the wearing of Saudi Arabian costumes and the rejection of African indigenous names in favour of Arab names, including the adoption of names specific to celebrated Arab Muslims of the past, are clear indications of this. Legends of origin of several West African peoples and dynasties have also claimed Arab roots, even in some cases non-Muslim roots, so great is the prestige of merely being of 'Arab' ancestry.[8] Despite the fact that Arabs now constitute no more than 15% of Muslims world-wide, they remain the dominant force within Islam by virtue of the fact that the Prophet of Islam was an Arab, the message he brought is couched in Arabic and the focal point of daily prayer, and annual pilgrimage, is in Arabia. Perhaps it is not irrelevant to add that in the 1980s some of the Arab countries—specifically Saudi Arabia and the Gulf states—have been among the wealthiest of all Muslim countries.

Much fuss has been made in the Western press about Iran's avowed aim to export Islamic revolution. Although the Ayatollah Khomeini and his supporters have certainly had a considerable impact on Muslims in the sense of heightening Muslim self-consciousness through defying the 'unbelievers' of the West and imbuing many with a willingness to die for the faith, their impact has not (at least so far) been as great as some western analysts once predicted, in part because of the Sunni-Shīʿī sectarian split and in part because many Sunni Muslims were horrified at Iranian militancy which disrupted the pilgrimage to Mecca on two occasions. In fact, Saudi Arabia, the arch-enemy of Iran, has been much more successful in a less obvious way in exporting its own Islamic ideology and thereby sowing the seeds of discord in Africa, both between Muslims and non-Muslims and between Muslims and Muslims. The austere teachings of the eighteenth century Arabian reformer Muḥammad b. ʿAbd al-Wahhāb[9] which form the basis of the Saudi Arabian way of life, both private and public, lay major emphasis on Islamic law—*sharīʿa*—as the basis of Islamic society and the elimination of what are termed, rather euphemistically, 'innovations'(*bidʿa*).[10] Among the things which these doctrines view as innovations is Sufism, the mystical path to God, which in its popular form, the Sufi Brotherhood or Path (*ṭarīqa*), is an important expression of the faith among millions of African Muslims. For them, adherence to the Tijāniyya, Qādiriyya or Murīdiyya Brotherhood is an integral part of their Islamic identity. Tensions and divisions have therefore arisen in several West African countries—notably Senegal, Mali and Nigeria—where doctrines propagated by the Saudi religious establishment have taken root and funds originating in Saudi Arabia have been channelled towards the building of separatist mosques and schools.[11]

But it is the notion of the fundamental importance of *sharīʿa* which holds out the possibility of the most dangerous kind of division—that between Muslims and non-Muslims. Indeed, it is the major point of contention in the renewed civil war in the Sudan. *Sharīʿa* is a thorny issue. Even the term itself is difficult to define. At its broadest it means 'the good Muslim life' as propounded by the Qur'an and as lived out by the Prophet Muḥammad and his original community. At its narrowest, it means strict adherence to Islamic law and this latter is in itself very hard to define. For many it means what was elaborated by the great scholars of the first five centuries of Islam and incorporated in treatises between the tenth and the fourteenth centuries, remaining scarcely changed since then. These treatises regulate, in theory, all aspects of the believer's life, including how he should perform his religious obligations, how he should marry, how his property should be disposed of on his death, etc. They also contain commercial codes and certain laws for which there are fixed and often very severe punishments, known as *ḥudūd* , including beating or stoning to death for sexual offences, amputation of a hand for theft, whipping for drinking alcohol, crucifixion and the amputation of limbs for rebellion and death for apostacy, heresy and blasphemy. When Muslims clamour for the right to be judged by *Sharīʿa* law, claiming it as one of their religious rights, as they did in Nigeria during debates on the constitution in 1977 and again in 1989, it is not always clear just how much of what *Sharīʿa* they want implemented. Some, such as the former Grand Khadi (*qadī*) of northern Nigeria, *Al-Ḥājj* Abubakar Gummi have openly advocated the implementation of *Sharīʿa* as the law of the land in Nigeria and the proclamation of an Islamic state. Non-Muslims are, not surprisingly, alarmed and outraged by such demands and the example of the Sudan makes it clear why they should be. Since the edict by Nimeiri in 1983 that *Sharīʿa* should be the sole law for the whole of the Sudan there have been amputations of hands, floggings for alcohol consumption and a hanging for apostacy.[12] This has led the non-Muslims in the Sudan (joined actively or passively by many Muslims) to oppose Sharīʿa to the point of rebellion and civil war. Nor is this all. There can be no doubt that Sharīʿa, as interpreted by the traditionalist Muslim jurisprudents—and no 'reformed' Sharīʿa has ever been universally accepted—makes Christians and Jews permitted to dwell in an Islamic state into second-class citizens, discriminated against at every level of their existence,[13] while heretics may be put to death (as witnessed by the fate of the Bahāʾīs in Iran and in the Sudanese case cited above)[14] and 'unbelievers' who fall outside those categories reduced to slavery. Christians in Nigeria have responded to what they see as a threat of Muslim domination and the possible imposition of such discriminatory laws by forming their own militant organisations, especially in the so-called Middle Belt on the frontiers between Christianity and Islam. The two fundamentalisms feed on one another and the resulting tensions often run high. An incident in 1987 led to widespread inter-faith clashes in more than one northern Nigerian city and the burning of churches, mosques, shops and other property as well as a number of deaths.[15] While it would be unfair to lay the blame for such outbursts of violence at the door of Saudi Arabia or any other Arab country, the encouragement given by Saudi Arabia to an uncompromising advocate of traditional *Sharīʿa*, like Abubakar Gummi (to whom the Saudis awarded the King Feisal Prize to counter-balance Wole Soyinka's award of the Nobel Prize for Literature) is bound to give certain signals to non-Muslim Nigerians, and indeed to all non-Muslim Africans and to further bolster stereotypes about both Islam and Arabs. None of this can be constructive for Arab-African dialogue and co-operation.

What, then, is the future of Arab-African relations? Fortunately I am a historian and not a prophet, so I so I hope I will not hold me hold accountable if some of my prognostications are not realised. Nevertheless, I would like to put forward some points which I think should be borne in mind when thinking about this question:

The first point to be borne in mind is that, geographically, about one third of the African continent is taken up by Arab nations and, if we accept the principles of the OAU, they are as much Africans as the non-Arab nations of the continent.

Secondly, on the political level the Sudan is a thought test for the future of Arab-African relations. If a *modus vivendi* can be found such as to accomodate the aspirations and calm the fears of both the non-Arab (and basically non-Muslim) and the 'Arab' (and almost wholly Muslim) sectors of the population, it can be a model for Arab/non-Arab and Muslim/non-Muslim relations in Africa. Failure will be fraught with dangers and far-reaching implications for the rest of sub-Saharan Africa, as much for countries where Muslims are in a minority as for countries where they are a majority.

Thirdly, if a solution can be found to the question of Palestintian rights and when South Africa achieves majority rule, the major regional political questions which absorb so much energy on either side can be released for more constructive purposes. Two irritants to better Arab-African relations will have been removed and neither side need accuse the other of lack of solidarity.

Finally if one thought that the future was uncertain globally during the period of the Cold War and the threat of nuclear conflagration, then this is nothing to what it seems now that detente has broken out between West and East, and eastern Europe and the Soviet Union are in the throes of revolutionary change. What will this, combined with the impending political integration of the European Community in 1992, mean for Africa and for the Arab World? And what will it mean for the relationship between them? What it seems likely to mean, as far as I can see, at any rate in the medium term, is that Europe will remain very turned in upon itself, trying to deal with the problems that will arise as Eastern European countries and the Soviet Union rebuild shattered economies and experiment with democratic freedoms. The United States is likely to want to play a role in this while at the same time paying increased attention to its own internal economic and social problems (drugs, AIDS, housing, education and workforce quality) so as to be in a stronger position when a united Europe (including no doubt eventually some of the present Eastern Bloc countries) emerges.

Will all this have some positive effect on relations between the Arab World and sub-Saharan Africa? Will they draw closer politically and economically and fulfill the destiny which Nasser envisaged for them in the 1950s? My own guess is that they will not. The countries of the Arab League are already engaged in serious discussions with the countries of the European Community on how to build a new economic relationship between the Arab World and Europe, despite their political differences, especially in view of the implications of European monetary and customs union in 1992. Some of them, with enormous investments in Europe, have a clear vested interest in the prosperity and stability of Europe while having little investment or potential interest in Africa. Africa, and more particularly West Africa, which is our primary concern in these lectures, will have to fight for its own piece of the pie and it will be in a far better position to do this if it can present a reasonably united front. For this African regional groupings, such as ECOWAS, will have to be strengthened and larger and freer markets established.[16] When Kwame Nkrumah wrote *Africa Must Unite*, he was thinking, first and foremost, of political unity and an eventual United States of Africa; such was the thinking a quarter of a century ago in the wake of liberation from alien occupation of African lands. Now, more than ever, the issue is economic unity in the face of massive world economic power blocks. The great wars of the twenty-first century will not be fought with missiles and nuclear weapons—they pose too great a threat to human existence. Rather the great wars will be fought with computers, commodities and currencies. Ghana will be—indeed already is—caught up in their opening skirmishes.

Part IV

Basil Davidson

His Biography and African Study Writings

Basil Davidson was born in England in 1914, and still lives there—near Bath, Somerset—reading and writing on Africa. I first met him in Ibadan in the early 1960s when I was teaching at the University of Ibadan, having set up a fully new department on the Arabic language and Islamic studies. I have met with him many times since then, both in West Africa and in England. Indeed, I was fortunate to see him at his Somerset house on his birthday on 9th November, 2005, and had the pleasure of showing him what I was writing for him.

He was originally a journalist and, in the the Second World War he produced for the British government information on Yugoslavia and Greece.[1] After various journalistic appointments, including work for *The Times*, as chief foreign leader writer, he began the systematic study of Africa in 1950, and soon specialized in the study of African history. He has travelled in Africa since 1951 and has accepted several invitations as visiting professor at universities seeking his scholarship (Ghana, 1964, U.C.L.A. 1965 and 1971, Edinburgh 1972). In 1974 he was appointed Honorary Research Fellow of the Centre of West African Studies, University of Birmingham, and a Senior Simm Research Fellow of the University of Manchester for 1975–6.

Basil Davidson has been a major publisher of books on Africa, and here is a list of works of his contained in the Africana Library of Northwestern University:[2]

Africa, History and Achievement, London: Commonwealth Institute, 1984.

Africa in History: Themes and Outlines New York: Macmillan, 1968, St. Albans: Paladin, 1974; revised and expanded, London: Paladin, 1984, London: Phoenix, 1992 (revised edition as *Africa: History of a Continent*; with photographs by Werner Forman, London, New York: Spring Books, 1972.

Africa: History of a Continenr, London: Weidenfeld & Nicholson, 1966

Africa in history: themes and outlines, London: Cape, 1955; St Albans:Paladin Books, 1974.

African Civilization Revisited: from Antiquity to Modern Times, Trenton [NJ]: Africa World Press, 1991.

The African Genius; an Introduction to African cultural and Social History, Boston: Little, Brown, 1970.

The African Awakening, London: Cape, 1955; New York: Macmillan, 1955. Trans. in Chinese: *Fei-chou ti chūI^eh hsing / Pai*-chÊ»i-erh Tai-wei-hsuÌ^n chu *; Shih Jen i*, Pei-ching :Shih chieh chih shih chÊ»u pan she, 1957.

African Nationalism and the Problems of Nation-Building, Lagos: Nigerian Institute of International Affairs, 1987.

The African past; chronicles from antiquity to modern times, Boston: Little, Brown, 1964; Harmondsworth: Penguin, 1966.

The Africans: an entry to cultural history, Harlow: Longmans, 1969, and 1973.

The African slave trade: precolonial history, 1450–1850, Boston: Little, Brown,1961.

Black Man's Burden: Africa and the Curse of the Nation State, Boston: Little, Brown, 1961.

The African Slave Trade , Boston: Little, Brown, 1980.

Old Africa Rediscovered, translated into French by Pierre Vidaud: *L'Afrique avant les blancs, découverte du passé oublié de l'Afrique*, Paris: Presses Universitaires de France, 1962.

Africa, Voyage of Discovery [videorecording] / written and presented by Basil Davidson ; executive producer, Mick Csaky ; director, Christopher Ralling ; a Mitchell Beazley Television RM ARTS/Channel Four co-production in association with the Nigerian Television Authority. Published: Chicago, c 1984.

Alle radici dell'Africa nuova / Basil Davidson ; intervista di Antonio Bronda, Roma: Editori riuniti, 1979.

Angola, 1961, the factual record, London: Union of Democratic Control, 1961(?).

L'Angola au coeur des tempêtes. Traduit de l'Anglais par Louis Rigaudia, Paris: F. Maspero, 1972.

Behind the war in Eritrea, edited by Basil Davidson, Lionel Cliffe, and Bereket Habte Selassie, Nottingham: Spokesman, 1980.

The Black Man's Burden: Africa and the curse of the nation-state, New York: Times Books, 1992.

Black mother! Africa: the years of trial, London: V. Gollancz, 1961; London: Longman, 1970.

Black mother; the years of the African slave trade, Boston:Little, Brown, 1961. *Black star; a view of the life and times of Kwame Nkrumah*, London, Allen Lane, 1973; New

York, Praeger, 1974; with a foreword by Ann Seidman, Boulder: Westview Press, 1989.

Can Africa survive? Arguments against growth without development, Boston: Little, Brown. 1974; London: Heinemann, 1975.

Can we write African history?, Los Angeles, 1965.

Crossroads in Africa: Basil Davidson talks to Antonio Bronda, Nottingham: Spokesman Books, 1980.

Daily mirror spotlight on the new Africa, London]: Daily Mirror Newspapers, 1960.

The darkening shadow over Africa, London: Union of Democratic Control, 1953.

Discovering Africa's Past, London: Longman, 1978.

Discovering our African heritage, Boston: Ginn, 1971.

L'Afrique avant les blancs, découverte du passé oublié de l'Afrique, French trans. by Pierre Vidaud, Paris: Presses iniversitaires de France, 1962.

The Fortunate Isles: a Study in African Transformation, London: Hutchinson, 1989.

A Guide to African Hstory, New York, 1969.

Modern Africa: a social and political history, 3rd edn., London; New York, 1994.

The Search for Africa: History, Culture, Politics, New York: Times Books, *c.* 1994.

Appendix I

INSTITUTE FOR THE STUDY OF ISLAMIC THOUGHT IN AFRICA (ISITA)

ISITA—IS-IT-A good program? Yes, I believe it is. It was set up by me, with the collaboration of Sean O'Fahey, in 2001, as a sector of the Program of African Studies at Northwestern University (Evanston, Illinois). Northwestern University has had focus on the study of Africa for the past fifty years, since Melville Herskovits set up a Program of African Studies and an "Africana" section of the university's library.

The principle objectives of ISITA are:

1. To preserve, and disseminate information on, African Arabic manuscript libraries.

2. To establish networks of collaboration between African, American, and European scholars working on the Islamic intellectual tradition in Africa.

3. To bring scholars together to discuss multiple aspects of Islamic Thought in Africa through workshops, colloquia and conferences.

4. To promote the publication of collective volumes of studies arising from scholarly meetings, and essential works of reference relating to the Islamic intellectual tradition in Africa.

One of our primary concentrations has been on the libraries of Timbuktu. We hope to help library owners to preserve their manuscripts scientifically, and to digitize them so that the contents of the library can be more widely available, and accessible to researchers without actually having to handle the manuscripts themselves.

ISITA has held annual conferences and some seminars, inviting scholars from African countries to spend time with ISITA and give papers on aspects of Islamic thought in Africa. Papers of such annual conferences so far have been published in volumes through the Brill 'Islam in Africa" series; and hopefully, more will come.

Brill has also taken responsibility for publication of other volumes relating to Islam in thought in Africa. That is the "Arabic Literature of Africa" (ALA) series that I set up, together with Sean O'Fahey long before the initiation of ISITA, though ALA became a central objective of ISITA from 2001. ALA was originally planned by me to cover only Arabic writings in West Africa, but in 1980 Sean O'Fahey suggested that it would be useful to cover other areas in sub-Saharan Africa(or "Sudanic Africa", lit. 'black' Africa), and that he was willing to deal with non-West Africa volumes, covering the Nile valley (modern Sudan Republic), the north-east area and the east coast of Africa. Hence, in 1994, he got published Volume I: "The Writings of Eastern Sudanic Africa to *c*, 1900", the chapters of which are:

1. The Sudanese Valley before 1820.
2. Chronicles and Related Materials.
3. The Writings of the Turkiyya.
4. (with Albrecht Hofheinz): Popular Poetry.
5. The Sammāniyya Tradition.
6. (with Yaḥyā Muḥammad Ibrāhīm): The Idrīsiyya Tradition.
7. (by Knut Vikør): The Sanūsiyya Tradition.
8. (with Albrecht Hofheinz and Bernd Radtke): The Khatmiyya Tradition.
9. (with Bernd Radtke): The Writings of Ismaʿīl al-Walī and his Descendants.
10. (by Albrecht Hofheinz): The Writings of the Majādhib
11. The Hindiyya, Qādiriyya, Saʿdiyya and Tijāniyya
12. (with Muḥammad Ibrāhīm Abū Salīm): The Writings of the Mahdiyya

In the next year (1995) Volume II: " The Writings of Central Sudanic Africa", compiled by me, with parts added to, or put together, by others, was published by Brill,[1] chiefly covering Nigeria. Its contents are:

1. The Central Sudan before 1800.
2. The Fodiyawa: (1) Shaykh ʿUthmān b. Muḥammad Fodiye.
3. The Fodiyawa: (2) ʿAbd Allāh b. Muḥammad Fodiye.
4. The Fodiyawa: (3) Muḥammad Bello.

5. Sokoto (1): Other Members of the Fodiyawa and the Wazirs.
6. Sokoto (2): Other Writers of the Nineteenth and Twentieth Centuries.
7. Kano since 1800 (1): Emirs and Writers of theTijāniyya Ṭarīqa.
8. (i, with Roman Loimeier): Kano since 1800 (ii): Writers of the Qādiriyya Ṭarīqa and Unaffiliated Writers.
9. Writers of Katsina, Zaria, Bauchi and Lokoja.
10. (with Hamidu Bobboyi): Bornu, Wadai and Adamawa.
11. (by Stefan Reichmuth and Razaq D. Abubakre): Ilorin and Nupe in the Nineteenth and Twentieth Centuries.
12. (by Stefan Reichmuth and Razaq D. Abubakre): Ibadan, Lagos and Other Areas of Southern Nigeria.
13. (with Muhammad Sani Umar): Polemical Literature for, and against, Sufism.
14. King-Lists, Chronicles, and Other Minor Historical Works

Volume III, divided into two parts (A & B), has been compiled by Sean O'Fahey: Volume IIIA covers Eritrea, Ethiopia and Somalia, and was published in 2004; Volume IIIB covers East Africa, including all writings in Swahili in the Arabic script, and is expected to be published early in 2006. Volume IV " The Writings of Western Sudanic Africa" was compiled by me, with some skilled assistants, and was published in 2003. Its contents are:

1. The Middle Niger to 1800.
2. The Middle Niger in the nineteenth and twentieth centuries.
3. The Saharan Fringes of Mali I: The Kunta.
4. The Saharan Fringes of Mali II: Other Writers of Azawād.
5. Central Mali in the Nineteenth and Twentieth Centuries.
6. (with Ousmane Kane & Rüdiger Seesemann): Senegambia i:The Niassene Tijānī Tradition.
7. (with Ousmane Kane): Senegambia ii: Other Tijānī Writers.
8. (with Ousmane Kane): Senegambia iii: Writers of the Murīd Ṭarīqa.
9. (with Ousmane Kane): Other Writers of the Senegambian Region.

10. (with Bernard Salvaing): Writers of Guinea.
11. Writers of Niger.
12. (with Ivor Wilks & Mark Sey): Writers of the Greater Voltaic Region.
13. Anonymous Chronicles, King-Lists and Historical Fragments, chiefly of Mali and Niger.

At the end is an Appendix on "Unassigned Writers".

Other volumes still under preparation are: ALA V, on writings in the Republic of Sudan in the twentieth century by Sean O'Fahey; and ALA VI, on writings of the Western Sahara, i.e. mainly Mauritania, by myself, with the assistance of Ulrich Rebstock and Charles Stewart. All volumes of ALA give brief biographies of authors of Arabic works, and information on the location of manuscripts of their writings, and–if in existence—publications of the Arabic texts and any translations—primarily into English or French, but if existent, into African languages such as Hausa or Fulani. If African authors of Arabic writings also wrote similar type of works in their own language, or in English or French, these are also listed. It is also hoped that a different volume can be put together of Arabic script writings in Hausa and Fulani–of which there have been many–principally prepared by Muhammad Sani Umar and Hamidu Bobboyi, both of whom are Nigerians, and graduates of Northwesterrn University, both of whom have made contributions to ISITA.

Appendix II

Sudanic Africa: A Journal of Historical Sources

The journal *Sudanic Africa* has been published annually since 1990. I was keen to have such a journal after producing the *Bulletin of Information* of the Fontes Historiae Africanae project, which I directed from 1973 to 1985.[1] After discussing this with Sean O'Fahey at the University of Bergen (Norway), we found that Knut Vikør of the Centre for Middle Eastern and Islamic Studies at that university was pleased to be the editor of it and arrange local publication annually. That journal has contained many Arabic documents of Africa with translations, and in vol. 13 of 2002 it was decided to publish similar type articles that had originally appeared in the *Bulletin of Information* between 1979 and 1987, since such copies of the *Bulletin of Information* are no longer available.. The *Bulletin* articles re-published in that *Sudanic Africa* volume—many on the Sudan—are :

1.	John O. Hunwick & R.S. O'Fahey:	Some *waqf* Documents from Lamu.
2.	Lidwien Kapteijns & Jay Spaulding:	Indian Ocean Diplomacy: Two Documents Relating to the Nineteenth-Century Mijertein Coast.
3.	Jay Spaulding & ʿAbd al-Ghaffār M. Aḥmad:	The Sinnār King-List of the *sīd al-qūm* Aḥmad, 1772
4.	Jay Spaulding:	A Charter of Sultan Bādī b. Nøl of Sinnār, 1145/1732–3

5.	Muʿtaṣim al-Shaykh al-ʿAbbās, ʿAlī ʿUthmān Muḥammad Ṣāliḥ and Jay Spaulding:	A Colophon from Eighteenth-Century Sinnār
6.	Neil McHugh:	Land, lords and Holy Men in Eighteenth-Century Sinnār: Two Documents
7.	Jay Spaulding:	Two Documents from the Days of Nāṣir b. Muḥammad Abū Lilaylik, Hamaj Regent of Sinnār
8.	R.S. O'Fahey:	A History of the Awlād Hindī
9.	John O. Hunwick:	a Mahdist Letter from Darfur
10.	R.S. O'Fahey, John O. Hunwick and D. Lange:	Two Glosses Concerning *bilād al-sūdān* on a Manuscript of al-Nuwayrī's *Nihāyat al-arab*
11.	ʿUmar al-Nagar:	The *Asānīd* of Shehu Dan Fodio: Hor Far are they a contribution to his Biography?
12.	John O. Voll:	ʿUthmān b. Muḥammad Fūdī's *sanad* to al-Bukhārī as presented in *Tazyīn al-waraqāt*
13.	Ivor Wilks & John O. Hunwick:	Samoriana
14.	John O. Hunwick:	West African Arab Manuscript Colophons: I Askiya Muḥammad Bānī's Copy of the *Risāla* of Ibn Abī Zayd
15.	John O. Hunwick:	West African Arab Manuscript Colophons: I; A Sixteenth-Century Copy of the *Muḥkam* of Ibn Sīdah
16.	Zahra Tamouth	Les sources sur la Qādiriyya Kuntiyya au XIXe siècle conservées dans les bibliothèques marocaines et françaises.

Appendix III

Conservation of West African Arabic Manuscripts

I, John Hunwick, have been very anxious to promote conservation of Arabic manuscripts from West Africa, and make knowledge of them available for other scholars. My first concern was in 1964 at the University of Ibadan (Nigeria), where I set up a "Centre of Arabic Documentation", getting manuscripts from the northern region of the country microfilmed and cataloged in an annual *Bulletin* of the Centre, together with articles on such topics. However, this did not apparently continue to occur after I left that university at the end of 1966. However, in 1967 I was invited to a Unesco meeting of "Experts on Arabic Sources of African History", held in Timbuktu. At the end of the conference I signed up with others on a recommendation to be sent to the government of Mali, asking them to set up a project for the conservation of Arabic manuscripts. So, in 1973, when the Mali government had obtained financial support, mainly from Kuwait, they built in Timbuktu what was called the "Centre de Documentation et de Recherche Historique Ahmed Baba [CEDRAB]" in Timbuktu, and got into it Arabic manuscripts, bought, or as gifts, from owners of manuscripts in the city, nowadays having a total of about 20,000 items. The original 9,000 manuscripts were later catalogued in five volumes published in London (all in Arabic) by the Al-Furqan Islamic Heritage Foundation (1996–1998). That Foundation has also published catalogs of other Arabic manuscript collections in West Africa; one is a 3-volume catalog of a private collection in Timbuktu: the 6,000 items of the Mamma Haidara Library, run by Abdul-Kader Ḥaidara, with manuscripts inherited from his father, who died in 1980. Interestingly, Abdul-Kader is to bring some of his manuscripts to the United States in Spring 2006 for an exhibition, to be held first at the International Museum of Muslim Cultures in Jackson, Mississipi, and then in the Du Sable Museum in Chicago in August 2006.

The Al-Furqan Islamic Heritage Foundation of London has also published catalogs of Arabic manuscripts from Nigeria, Niger, and Senegal:

1. *The Nigerian National Archives of Kaduna* (1645 items), edited and annotated by myself; 1 vol., 1997.
2. *The University of Ibadan Library* (422 items), also edited and annotated by myself; 1 vol., 2001.
3. *Handlist of Manuscripts in the Libraries of Shaykh Serigne Mor Mbaye Cissé, al-Ḥājj Malick Sy & Shaykh Ibrāhīm Niasse, of Senegal* (804 items), compiled and edited by Ousmane Kane, 1 vol., 1997.
4. *Catalogue of Islamic Manuscripts at the Institut des Recherches en Sciences Humaines, Niamey* (2003 items), prepared by Hassane Moulay, 4 vols, 2005.

In Nigeria there are also public collections of Arabic manuscripts in Jos, Kaduna, Kano, Sokoto, and Maiduguri (Bornu); and also African Arabic manuscript collections in the University libraries of Ibada, Lagos, Dakar. and in the Africana Library of Northwestern University, Evanston [IL] (where I was a professor, 1981–2004), with several collectiond: the ʿUmar Falke collection from Kano (3,500 mss.); a collection of 400 mss. obtained from varios places in northern Nigeria by John Paden, the former director of the Program of African Studies at Northwestern University; the John Hunwick collection—mainly published manuscripts from northern Nigeria and from Senegal [i.e. handwritten works photocopied into paper-bound little 'books']—a total of 550 items. The manuscript collection of the Africana Library also now contains printed copies of some 450 manuscripts from a photocopied collection of Arabic manuscripts in the African Studies Program of the University of Ghana, Legon (near Accra). That project was directed by Ivor Wilks when he taught at the University of Ghana, and in 1993 (upon retirement at Northwestern University) he donated his copies to the Africana Library.

In conclusion, I would like to make known the published work that I have produced on "Arabic Literature of Africa"—that being two large volumes on authors of West Africa and their Arabic writings in manuscripts, or as such Arabic texts have been published or translated.[1] These are volumes 2 and 4 of a larger series, on which Sean O'Fahey is also working (on the eastern half of Africa):

Vol. II: "The Writings of Central Sudanic Africa" principally covers Nigeria, including information of such manuscripts now preserved far away from that country, for example in Morocco, Algeria, Egypt, Turkey, Saudi Arabia, France, England, and America. It was published by Brill in 1995, 732 pages, including indexes of "Authors", "Titles", "First Lines of Poetry", and a "General Index" containing any other useful matters. For chapter titles, see p. 113 in Appendix 1 above.

Vol IV: "The Writings of Western Sudanic Africa" covers:

1 & 2: 'The Middle Niger" (mainly Timbuktu).
3 & 4: The Saharan Fringes of Mali ("The Kunta" and "Other Writers of Azawad".
5: Central Mali in the nineteenth and twentieth Centuries.
6, 7, 8, 9: Senegambia (The Niassene Tijānī Tradition; other Tijānī Writers; Writers of the Murīd *Ṭarīqa*; Other writers of the Senegambian Region).
10. Writers of Guinea.
11. Writers of Niger.
12. Writers of the Greater Voltaic Region (i.e, N. Ghana and neighboring areas of Ivory Coast and Burkina Faso)
13. Anonymous Chronicles, King-Lists, and Historical Fragments, chiefly of Mali and Niger.

Published by Brill, 2003 [814 pages, with types of indexes similar to those in Vol. IIA].

Volumes I & III (A & B), and V, prepared by Sean O'Fahey, cover other —eastern—areas of sub-Saharan Africa: I, the Nile valley to 1900, IIIA, Ethiopia, Somalia, IIIB Eastern Africa [Kenya and Tanzania], AND Vol. VI: Sudan in the twentieth century.

With Arabic as "the Latin of Africa", volumes also include some information on manuscripts in African languages in the Arabic script by those who were principally writers in Arabic: in Vol. II: Hausa, Fulfulde, and Yoruba or Nupe; Vol. IV: Fulfulde, Hausa, Songhay, and Wolof; Vol. IIIB: Swahili. Later, other volumes of African languages in the Arabic script are to be planned; first of all, Hausa and Swahili works from authors in Nigeria and Cameroun.

Finally, I am working to produce Volume VI: "Writings of the Western Sahara", mainly covering Mauritania, where a great deal of Arabic writing has been done.

To promote interest in Arabic manuscripts and other matters, in 2001 I set up an "Institute for the Study of Islamic Thought in Africa"[ISITA], as a sector of Northwestern University's Program of African Studies; see Appendix 1. In honor of my work on Arabic manuscripts, in November 2005 some Timbuktu scholars set up in thrir city the "Club John O. Hunwick". Among its objectives they called for "Initiation des jeunes à la recherche, la collecte, et la restauration des anciens manuscrits de Tombouctou."

Appendix IV

Northwestern Published Manuscripts

Over several research visits to Kano and Dakar, I purchased a number of published handwritten /manuscript Arabic works by local Muslim scholars. These items were then placed into the Arabic manuscript room of the Africana section of the Northwestern University Library; and became known as the "Hunwick Collection". They all cover many different topics, and some are sold in local markets, or small specialised stores. So here is a list of some of those items, clearly showing the keenness of local Arabic writing and reading.

NU/Hunwick, 83: AL-ṬĀHIR b. IBRĀHĪM b. HĀRŪN b. MĀLIK al-Fullānī (or -Fallātī) al-Barnāwī al-Tārazī al-Fayrammī, known as Ḍahiru Feroma (d. after 1745–6): *al-Durar al-Lawāmiʿ li-ahlihi ʿalā manār al-jāmiʿ*. 796 vv. on grammar. Opens: *al-Ḥamdu li'llāhi 'lladhī taṣarrafā * Fī fiʿlihi bi-ḥikmitin taʿarrafā..* 796 verses in 72 pages. Book prepared by Sulaymān b, ʿAlū in 1387/ 1967–8, and published in Sokoto

NU/Hunwick, 125:ʿUTHMĀN b. MUḤAMMAD FODIYE: Majmūʿ al-arbaʿa kutub: (1)Tanbīh al-ghāfilīn.; by Asmāʾ bt. Sh. ʿUthmān, (2) Dawāʾ al-waswās.; by ʿAbd Allāh b. Muḥammad Fodiye (3) Wathīqat al-Shaykh ʿUthmān b. Fūdī (addressed to an itinerant teacher of tafsīr), (4) Asmāʾ al-rusul..

NU/Hunwick, 126: ʿabdullĀh b. MUḤAMMAD b. ʿuthmĀn Ibn FŪDĪ: Majmūʿa al-kutub al-thalātha al-mufīda.The three books are: (1) ʿUmdat al-ʿulamāʾ. (2) ʿUmdat al-mutaʿabbidīn wa l-muḥtarifīn. (3) ʿAlāmāt al-mutaʿbbidīn li-sunnat al-rasūl—ṣallā 'llāhu ʿalayji wa-sallam—min al-rijāl wa 'l-nisāʾ.

NU/Hunwick, 351: MUḤAMMAD b. MASANIH b. ʿUMAR b. MUḤAMMAD b. ʿABD

ALLĀH b. NŪḤ al-Barnāwī al-Kashināwī, known as Δan Masanih (d. 1667): Mazjarat al-fityān ʿalā ṭafʾ nūr Allāh bi'l-ʿiṣyān [Homilectic poem of 48 vv.]

NU/Hunwick, 351: MUḤAMMAD b. AL-ṢABBĀGH b. MUḤAMMAD b. AL-ḤĀJJ b. BARAKA b. IBRĀHĪM al-Kashnāwī al-ʿArabī, known as Ibn al-Ṣabbāgh, and in Hausa as Δan Marina (fl. 1640–1): Mazjarat al-fityān ʿalā ṭafʾ nūr Allāh bi'l-ʿiṣyān. [Homilectic poem of 48 vv.]

NU/Hunwick, 424: MuḤammad b. MUḤAMMAD b. Ḥabīb AllĀh, known as aḤmadu bamba khadīm al-rasŪl (d. 1927): Muqaddimāt al-amdāḥ fī Mazāyā al-miftāḥ. Published in Dakar: Imprimerie Serigne Niang.

NU/Hunwick, 456: MuḤammad b. MUḤAMMAD b. Ḥabīb AllĀh: Nūr al-dārayn fī khidmat al-ḥāmī ʿan al-ʿārayn. Book of 306 pp.n praise of the Prophet Muḥammad; published in Dakar: Imprimerie Serigne Mbacké.

Notes

Chapter One

1. R. Nicolai, *Parentés linguistiques (à propos du Songhay)*, Paris: Éditions du CNRS, 1990.
2. See Section 6 below
3. Read 'Qamar' (?)—'moon', *cf.* Ptolemy's "Mons Lunae".
4. al-Idrısı, *Opus Geographicum*, ı, 32–3. (My translation above).
5. A collection cataloged and published as *Inventaire de la Bibliothèque* 'Umarienne de Ségou, Paris:Éditions du Centre Nationale de la Recherche Scientifique, 1985, in the *Fontes Historiae Africanae* [Subsidia Bibliographica, II].
6. Or 'Tombouctou' as the French called and spelt it.
7. The principal flood season is from September to March, especially in the Inland Delta, where a zone approximately 300 miles long and 150 miles wide is fully covered over with water.

Chapter Two

1. Some settled in the Sahel (*sāḥil*—lit. 'sea-shore', as if the Sahara were like an ocean).and the different languages that they now speak are in a group called the Nilo-Saharan languages; e.g. Fur, Kanuri, Songhay.
2. On cowries, see my 'Islamic financial institutions: theoretical structures and some of their practical applications in sub-Saharan Africa', in *Currencies, Credit and Culture: African Financial Insitutions in Historical Perspective*, ed. Endre Stiansen & Jane Guyer, Uppsala: Nordiska Afrikainstututet, 72–99
3. On the palace see Gūlrū Necipoğlu, *Architechture, Ceremonial and Power: the Topkapi Palace in the Fifteenth and Sixteenth Centuries*, Oxford University Press, 1993.
4. However, in the 1990s *sharī'a* (Islamic [Māikī] law) became the dominant legal force in much of northern Nigeria.
5. Yoruba Muslims also wrote their language in the Arabic script in the nineteenth century. See also below, Section 6:Arabic as the Latin of Africa.
6. See Section 7 below, pp. 76–77.

7. See Hopkins and Levtzon (1987). [sp?]
8. See The Travels of Ibn Baṭṭūṭa, Vol IV, trans. H. A. R. Gibb and C. Beckingham, Hakluyt Society: London, 1994.

Chapter Three

1. See Section 6 below.
2. In his Bayān wujūb al-hijra ʿalā ʾl-ʿibād; see translation by F.H. El Masri in the Fontes Historiae Africanae: Series Arabica, 1, Khartoum University Press & Oxford University Press , 1978, pp. 49–51, 87, 119, with reference to al-Kashf wa ʾl-bayān li-aṣnāf majlūb al-sūdān, an alternative title for Aḥmad Bābā's Miʿrāj al-ṣuʿūd ilā nayl ḥukm mujallab al-sūd—a work on slavery published and translated by John Hunwick & Fatima Harrak, Rabat: Institute of African Studies, University Mohammed V, 2000
3. On them all and their writings see ALA II, chapters 2–4..
4. See ALA II, 162–172.
5. ALA IV covers such Arabic writings.
6. Ed. and trans. by Fatḥi Ḥasan al-Maṣrī, Oxford University Press, 1978 [Fontes Historiae Africanae: Series Arabica, 1]
7. Ed Bahija Chadli, Rabat, 1996.

Chapter Four

1. Amadia is a location on the banks of the R. Niger to the west of Kabara. In Arabic it is spelled: Amaẓagha.
2. ʿAbd al-Raḥmān al-Saʿdī, *Taʾrīkh al-Sūdān*, Arabic text ed. O. Houdas, 1898, repr. 1964, 20–21; trans. J. O. Hunwick, *Timbuktu and the Songhay Empire*, Leiden, 1999, 29.
3. See Hunwick (1999), 35.
4. The origin of his family was from Andalusia, and then they moved to Morocco. Al-Ḥasan b. Muḥammad travelled a great deal in North Africa, and twice in West Africa in the early sixteenth century. And after his travel to Egypt, anmd on his way back to Morocco in 1518, he was captured by Sicillian corsairs in his ship in the Mediterranean. They took him to Rome where they presented him to Pope Leo X like a slave. A year later the Pope baptized him and gave him his own name (Leo). Later the name "Africanus" was added to that. He remained in Rome for a long time, and wrote a book in Italian called *Discrittione dell'Africa*, which was published in 1550 as Part 7 of the book *Delle navigationi e viaggi*, compiled by G.B. Ramusio. There is an English translation of descriptions of his travels in West Africa in Hunwick (1999).
5. Called in Songhay: Jingere Bēr.
6. The *Mukhtaṣar* is a famous book on law in the Mālikī *madh'hab*.

7. The book is a supplement to *al-Dībāj al-mudhahhab* by Ibn Farḥūn.
8. See *Nayl al-Ibtihāj*, 1st edn., Cairo, 1351/ 1932–3, p. 93 .
9. See below Ch. 6, p. 52.
10. Heinrich Barth, a German scholar, visited Timbuktu, on behalf of the British, in 1853, after traveling through northern Nigeria.
11. See Muḥammad al-Ṣaghī al-Ifrānī, *Nuzhat al-ḥādī bi-akhbār al-qarn al-ḥādī*, Casablanca, 1998, 171.
12. See Maḥmūd Kaʿti, *Taʾrīkh al-fattāsh*, Paris, 1913, 108.
13. See J.O. Hunwick, "West African Manuscript Colophons, II: A Sixteenth-Century Timbuktu Copy of the *Muḥkam* of Ibn Sīda", *Bulletin d'Information* (Fontes Historiae Africanae), 9/10 (1985/6), 49–69.
14. See Muḥammad al-Ṣaghīr al-Ifrānī, *Nuzhat al-ḥādī bi-akhbār mulūk al-qarn al-ḥādī*, Casablanca, 1998, p. 172.
15. Ed. Fāṭima Ḥarrāq, Rabat, 2000 (Université Mohamed V: Publications de l'Institut des Études Africaines); English translation in the same publication by John Hunwick.
16. Often known as "al-Takrūr".
17. This manuscript is preserved in Timbuktu nowadays in a private library under the direction of Ismael Diadié Haidara, who permitted me to publish this page of sale and translate it; see *Sudanic Africa*, xii (2001), pp. 111–114.
18. Published, edited by al-Hādī al-Mabrūk al-Dālī, Ṭarāblus, 2001.
19. I was considered to be such an "expert", and I went to Timbuktu for my first time in 1967.
20. Ismael Diadié Haidara, often went to Spain and taught there.
21. Arabic grammar by Muḥammad b. Muḥammad b. Dāwūd al-Ṣanhājī, d. 1323.
22. Published again in the book: *Les bibliothèques du désert: recherches et études sur un millénaire d'écrits*, Contributions réunies et présentés par Attilio Gaudio, Paris: L'Harmattan, 2002, pp. 287–303.

Chapter Five

1. Full title *Nayl al-ibtihāj bi-taṭrīz al-Dībāj*, published in Cairo, 1932 in margins of *al-Dībāj al-mudhahhab* by Ibrāhīm al-Mālikī [known as Ibn Farḥūn].
2. *Nayl al-ibtihāj*, 341.
3. Saḥnūn ʿAbd al-Salām b. Saʿīd b. Ḥabīb al-Tanūkhī; see GAL, S I, 299.
4. I record here my gratitude to Ismael Diadié Haidara, the man responsible for this library—now designated the Fondo Kati—for letting me see some items and take notes and photos.
5. See *Sudanic Africa*, 11 (2001), 111–114.
6. See Appendix 1 below.
7. In 2003, Ismael Diadié Haidara had a library building [Fondo Kaʿti] set up, through finance from Spain.
8. Centre de Documentation et de Recherche Historique Ahmed Baba.

9. *Handlist of Manuscripts in the Centre de Documentation et de Recherches Historiques Ahmed Baba, Timbuktu*, 5 vols., 1995–1998.
10. *Wuḍū'* is ablution before performing prayer (*ṣalāt*), obligatory in Islam.
11. See details in Appendix I below.
12. Through the Al-Furqān Foundation in London.
13. He took time at Northwestern University, 2000–2005 and then re-assumed his position at the University of Bergen (Norway).

Chapter Six

1. A translation of that Arabic text can be seen in Chapter 2 of my *Jews of a Saharan Oasis*, Princeton: Markus WienerPublishers, 2006.
2. In fact, for the Muslim Arabs to get some 400 slaves per year from up the R. Nile, but sending grain and textiles to the Nubian rulers who provided the slaves; this exchange, beginning in the 640s, lasted for several centuries
3. Also a group that became the 'Tuareg' moved into the Sahara from southern Libya.
4. Notably 'Umar b. Sa'īd, brought to S. Carolina in 1907, and later wrote an autobiography in Arabic, staying in America for all the rest of his life: see http://www.uib.no/jais/v005/Hunwick1WMd.pdf
5. The five daily prayers obligatory to serious Muslims are; at dawn; at mid-day; in mid-afternoon; at sunset; and in mid-evening. Verses of the Qur'ān must be recited in their original Arabic language.
6. Oxford University Press [for the British Academy], New York, 2003 [Fontes Historiae Africanae, New Series, 'Sources of African History, 4].
7. His book: *Al-Dībāj al-mudhahhab fī ma'rifat a'yan 'ulama' al-madh'hab.*
8. See *Nayl al-Ibtihāj*, 1st edn., Cairo, 1351/ 1932–3, p. 92.
9. Ed. and trans. by the Sudanese scholar Fatḥi Ḥasan al-Maṣrī, Oxford University Press, 1978 [Fontes Historiae Africanae: Series Arabica, 1]
10. Trans. Mervyn Hiskett, Ibadan University Press, 1963
11. Ed Bahija Chadli, Rabat, 1996.
12. Jean Boyd & Beverly B. Mack, *Collected Works of Nana Asmā', Daughter of Usman ɗan Fodyo (1793–1864)*, Michigan State University Press, 1997, pp. 191–3.
13. Manuscript in CEDRAB, 769.
14. Ms. NU/Hunwick, 475.
15. See in Appendix 1 on ISITA.. Sean O'Fahey is also producing similar volumes on the Sudan and East Africa.
16. Found and published by A.D. H. Bivar of S.O.A.S.
17. Both of those Nigerians did their Ph.D.s with me at Northwestern University.

Chapter Seven

1. On "Arab Views of Black Africans and Slavery", see Section 8.
2. See Appendix 3.

3. Hopkins & Levtzion (1981), 68.
4. *Ibid*: "There are also pretty slave girls with white complexions, good figures, firm breasts, slim waist, fat buttocks, wide shoulders and sexual organs so narrow that one of them may be enjoyed as though she were a virgin indefinitely"[Al-Bakrī's description].
5. Hopkins (1958), 78.
6. Ibn ʿIdhārī, *al-Bayān al-mughrib fī akhbār al-Andalus wa'l-Maghrib*, Beirut, n.d., i, 123; Hopkins, (1958), 72. Brett (1978), 529, argues that such slaves were more likely Slavs than Black Africans.
7. On this see also Levtzion (1985).
8. Brett, *op. cit,. loc. cit.*
9. Ibn Baṭṭūṭa (1994), iv, 975.
10. See the *Miʿrāj al-ṣuʿūd* of Aḥmad Bābā, annotated and translated by John Hunwick & Fatima Harrak, Rabat: Publications of the Institute of African Studies, University Mohammed V, 2001.
11. Idem, 44.
12. Idem, 45.
13. See Section 8 on this issue.
14. See Hunwick and Troutt Powell (2002), 6 (*ḥadīth* 693).
15. See Hunwick (1999), 258.
16. Abun Nasr (1987), 237; see also Hunwick & Troutt Powell (2002), 139–43.
17 Daumas (1860), 244.
18. On the definition of *jinn*, see article "*Djinn*" in *Encyclopaedia of Islam*, 2nd edn., Leiden:Brill, vol. II (1965), 546.
19. His treatise is called *Hatk al-sitr ʿammā ʿalayhi sūdān Tūnis min al-kufr*, and it has been published by ʿAbd al-Jalīl al-Tamīmī in his *Dirāsāt fīʾl-taʾrīkh al-ʿarabī al-Ifrīqī*, Zaghouan, 1994, 74–88.
20. A.J.N. Tremearne, *The Ban of the Bori. Demons and Demon Dancing in West and North Africa*, London, 1914, repr. 1968.
21. Ibn Khaldūn, *Kitāb al-ʿIbar*, in Hopkins and Levtzion (1981), 323.
22. I.e. gold of weight 2,805 lbs., and worth (now) about $13 million.
23. See Hunwick (1974), 113.
24. From *Nuzhat al-Ḥādī fī akhbār mulūk al-qarn al-ḥādī* of al-Ifrānī; see my article in *Sudanic Africa*, 1 (1990), 85–89.
25. From al-Saʿdī, *Taʾrīkh al-Sūdān* in Hunwick (1999), 52–3.
26. *Idem*, 56–7.
27. See Hunwick (1984).
28. Cl. Meillassoux, J.-L. Triaud, and John Hunwick, 'La géographie du Soudan d'après al-Bakri: trois lectures' in J.P. Chrétien et al, (1982) pp. 402–428; the Hunwick paper is in English, pp. 417–424. See also *Kitāb al-Maghrib fī dhikr bilād Ifrīqiya wa'l-Maghrib* by al-Bakrī, Alger: Imprimerie du Gouvernement, 1857.
29. See *Description de l'Afrique Septentrionale*, Texte arabe, ed. B. De Slane, Alger: Imprimerie du Gouvernment, 1857.
30. See Youssouf Kamal (1987), vol. iv, 91–128 [Edrisi]. See also *Opus Geographicum*,

Napoli-Romae, 1970, Pt. 1. The book was written for the ruler of Sicily, where al-Idrīsī spent part of his life; and it was first published in Rome in 1592, and translated into Italian in 160031.

31. See J. O. Hunwick, "The mid-fourteenth century capital of Mali", *Journal of African History*, xiv, 2 (1973), 195–208.
32. On all his travel in West Africa, see Hopkins & Levtzion (1981), 279–304.
33. Ibn Baṭṭūṭa (1994), iv, 975.
34. Jews of Touat had done trans-Saharan trading, together with Muslims; see Hunwick (2006) for all about them.
35. Published, with the title *Tāj al-Dīn fī mā yajib ʿalā ʾl-mulūk*, with an English translation by T. H. Baldwin, Beirut, 1932; see ALA II, 23–4 (item 21
36. See Hunwick (1984), which gives the Arabic text and translations of the Askiya's questions.
37. English translations of his West African travels are in Hunwick (1999), 272–291.
38. On this city see Angelo Piccioli, trans.Angus Davidson,*The Magic Gate of the Sahara*, London: Methuen & Co., 1935, pp. 209–299.

Chapter Eight

1. Qurʾān, 33: 50.
2. Qurʾān, 33: 50.
3. Quoted in Muḥammad al-Sanūsī al-Jārimī, *Tanbīh ahl al-ṭuhghyān ʿalā ḥurriyyat al-sūdān*, MS 1575, CEDRAB, Timbuktu.
4. *Ibid*
5. This may be compared to French and Portuguese policies of 'assimilation', ultimately based on Roman models, which conferred political rights on individual colonial subjects who achieved certain standards of education within the conquering power's system.
6. B. Lewis, 'The African Diaspora and the Civilization of Islam', in M.I. Kilson & R.I. Rotberg, *The African Diaspora* (Harvard University Press, 1976), 48–9.
7. ʿAbduh Badawī, *al-Shuʿarāʾ al-ṣud* (Cairo, 1973), 223–4.
8. Badawī, *op. cit.*, 123–4. The poet is al-Hayquṭan.
9. In Quṭayba, *Kitāb al-Maʿārif*, n L.E.Kubbel & V.V. Matveev, *Arabskiye istochniki,* vol. i, Moscow-Leningrad, 1960, 21.
10. The brothers being Shem and Japheth. Shem is considered to be the ultimate ancestor of the Arabs, and Japheth of the Europeans .
11. Ibn Khaldūn, however, does not seem to have rejected the genealogical explanation for the "origins" of African peoples. In his *Kitāb al-ʿıbar*, to which the *Muqaddima* forms an introduction, he names Ḥabash, Nūba and Zanjī as sons of Kūsh [b. Kanʿān] b. Nūḥ, on the authority of al-Masʿūdī and Ibn ʿAbd al-Barr. See the Beirut edition of 1956–61, iv, 410.
12. Ibn al-Faqīh al-Hamadhānī, *Mukhtaṣar kitab al-buldan*, ed. M.J. De Goeje, Leiden,

1885, 162. Translation by self, partly based on that of Bernard. Lewis in his *Islam from the Prophet Muḥammad to the Capture of Constantinople*, Oxford, 1987, ii, 209.

13. See Shams al-Dīn Mụhammad b. Abī̤ Tālib al-Dimashqī, *Nukhbat al-dahr fī ʿajāʾib al-barr wa ʾl-bạhr*, ed. A. Mehren, Leipzig, 1923, 15–17.
14. Idem, 273.
15. An early tenth century encyclopaedist who actually visited East Africa.
16. A philosopher and contemporary of Masʿūdī .
17. I.e.Galen, a 2nd century Greek physician.
18. Ibn Khaldūn, *Kitāb al-ʿibar*, i, 169–70.
19. Idem, i, 168–9.
20. Idem, i, 172.
21. Of. the conclusions reached by Drissa Diakité, reviewing medieval Arab authors writing about black Africa: "[L]a religion, les coutumes et moeurs des peuples Sudan [sont] généralement présentées . . . comme une négation de la vie, sans valeur, signe d'ignorance, de sauvagerie, de malédiction divine. Les valeurs réelles suivent les traces de l'Islam qui . . . élève les Sudan . . . au nombre des hommes civilisés. [L]es Sudan n'ont acquis les vertus fondementales de l'Homme que par l'influence du monde arabo-islamique." See his "Le 'pays des noirs' dans le récit des auteurs arabes anciens', *Notre Librairie*, 95 (oct-déc. 1988), 16–25.
22. Arabic: *muʾadhdhin* = 'prayer-caller'.
23. Al-Suyūṭī, *Nuzhat al-ʿumr fīʾl-tafḍīl bayn al-bīḍ waʾl-sūd waʾl-sumr,* Cairo, n.d.,44. Poet is Muḥammad b. Yūnus al-Bīsānī.
24. Quoted in ʿAbduh Badawī, *al-Sud waʿl-̣haḍara al-ʿarabiyya* ['Blacks and Arab Culture'] , Cairo, 1976, 161. The poet is Yaʿqūb b. Rāfiʿ,
25. See El-Said Badawi & Martin Hinds, *A Dictionary of Egyptian Arabic* (p. 559), Beirut: Librairie du Liban, 1986.

Chapter Nine

1. Originally a talk at the J.B. Danqual Memorial Lectures: Series 23, in Accra, February 1990, and then published with my other talks on the occasion; see Hunwick (1991a). 36–53.
2. In an article entitled 'West Africa before Europe' published in the Journal of the African Society, 2 (1902–3), he wrote (pp. 372–3): '[Islam], in its general lines, is much more suited to the African than any form of Christianity which has been presented for his acceptance...Indeed, Islam is the form that Christianity takes in Africa'.
3. See the official English translation, published by Information Department of the United Arab Republic, Cairo, n.d., 70.
4. Issue of 21 June 1974, quoted in Mohamed Omer Beshir, Terramedia: Issues in Afro-Arab Relations, Khartoum: Khartoum University Press and London: Ithaca Press, 1982, pp. 129–30.

5. Organization of African Unity.
6. Beshir, op. cit., 139.
7. After this lecture was delivered, a union between Libya and the Sudan was announced. Accords were signed in Tripoli on 2 March 1990. One of the benefits to Libya of this union is that it will have easier 'back-door' access to Chad. Darfur has for some time been a springboard for anti-Habré, pro-Ghadafi forces operating in eastern Chad.
8. E. g. the Sayfuwa dynasty of Kanem-Bornu which claimed descent from the pre-Islamic South Arabian hero Sayf b. Dhī Yazan, or the Yoruba whom Muslim writers have sometimes claimed to be descended from the pre-Islamic Yaʿrub b. Qaḥṭān.
9. His school of thought is often called 'Wahhābism' by western writers. Its practitioners describe themselves as muwaḥḥidūn —'those who uphold God's unity', the implication being that other Muslims do not, and hence are tainted with the mortal sin of shirk —'polytheism'.
10. In Arabic the term bidʿa has very negative connotations (unlike the English word 'innovation'), signifiying practices or beliefs that have no sanction in the Qurʾan, the sayings of the Prophet or the consensus of the early Muslim community.
11. On the tensions thus created in Nigeria, see Muhammad Sani Umar, 'Sufism and Anti-Sufism in Nigeria', M.A. dissertation, Bayero University (Kano), 1988.
12. The late Ustādh Maḥmūd Muḥammad Tāha, founder of a reformist group called the Republican Brothers, was executed on 18 January 1985. His teachings are set forth in his The Second Message of Islam , trans, Abdullahi An-Na'im, Syracuse University Press, 1987.
13. See Abdullahi An-Na'im, 'Religious Minorities under Islamic Law and the Limits of Cultural Relativism', Human Rights Quarterly (Johns Hopkins University), 9, i (1987).
14. A strict interpretation of (mediaeval and as yet unabrogated) Sharīʿa considers the Bahāʾīʾs heretics because their founder was a Muslim who claimed new (post-Muḥammad) divine inspiration. Blasphemy is also punishable by death—hence the Ayatollah Khomeini's ruling against Salman Rushdie.
15. The origins of the trouble are said to have lain in an attempt by a preacher, newly converted to Christianity from Islam, to give his own interpretation of certain passages of the Qurʾan.
16. This implies reasonable political stability and some African perestroika.

Basil Davidson Biography and Writings

1. He wrote *Special Operations Europe—Scenes from the Anti-Nazi war* first published by Gollancz in 1980.
2. See also: Christopher Fyfe (ed.), *African Studies since 1945: a Tribute to Basil Davidson: proceedings of a seminar in honour of Basil Davidson's sixtieth birthday, at*

the Centre of African Studies under the chairmanship of George Shepperson, London; Longman, 1976.

Appendix I

1. The Fontes project still exists, now directed by Prof. Viera Pawlikova-Vilhanov of the Slovak Academy of Sciences in Bratislava, Slovakia.

Appendix II

1. For more details of the contents of these volumes, see Appendix 1 above.

Appendix III

1. For more details of the contents of these volumes, see Appendix 1 above.

Bibliography

Aḥmad Bābā, *Nayl al-Ibtihāj bi-taṭrīz al-Dībāj*, in margins of *Kitāb al-Dībāj al-mudhah-hab fī Ma'rifat A'yān 'Ulama' al-Madh'hab* by Burhān al-Dīn Ibrāhīm b. 'Alī b. Muḥammad b. Farḥūn al-Ya'murī al-Madanī al-Mālikī, Cairo, 1351/1932.

——, *Mi'rāj al-ṣu'ūd ilā nayl ḥukm mujallab al-sūd*, edited text with translation by John Hunwick & Fatima Harrak, Rabat: Institute of African Studies, University Mohammed V, 2000.

ALA—*Arabic Literature of Africa*, vols. 1–4, ed, John Hunwick & R.S. O'Fahey, Leiden: Brill, 1994–2005.

Brett (1978), "The Arab Conquest and the rise of Islam in North Africa", in *Cambrifge History of Africa*, vol. 2, 490–555.

Chrétien, J.P. et al. (1982), *2000 Ans d'histoire africaine: le sol, la parole et l'écrit. Mélanges en hommage à Raymond Mauny*, Paris: Société Français d'Outre-mer.

Encyclopaedia of Islam, 11 vols, Leiden: Brill, 1960–2003.

GAL—*Geschichte der Arabischen Litteratur*, by Carl Brockelmann, 2 vols. +3 vols Supplement, Leiden: E.J. Brill, 1943–1949.

Holt, P.M. & Daly, M.W. *The History of the Sudan, from the Coming of Islam to the Present Day*, Boulder [CO]: Westview Press, 1979.

Hopkins, J. F. P. (1958), *Medieval Muslim government in Barbary until the sixth century of the Hijra*, London: Luzac.

——& Levtzion, N. (1981), *Corpus of Early Arabic Sources for West African History*, Cambridge University Press, 1981 [Fontes Historiae Africanae, Series Arabica IV].

Hunwick, John (1973), "The mid-fourteenth century capital of Mali", Journal of African History, xiv, 2 , 195–208.

—— (1977), 'Arabic language and Muslim Society in West Africa: a historical perspective", Ghana Social Science Journal , iv, 2 , 1–20.

—— (1984), "Ṣāliḥ al-Fullānī (1752/3–1803): The career and teachings of a West African 'Ālim in Medina", in A.H. Green (ed.), In Quest of an Islamic Humanism: Arabic and Islamic Studies in memory of Mohamed al-Nowaihi, Cairo: American University in Cairo Press, 1984, 139–153.

—— (1985), *Sharī'a in Songhay: the Replies of al-Maghīlī to the Questions of Askia Al-Ḥājj Muḥammad*, Oxford University Press [Fontes Historiae Africanae, Series Arabica, V]

—— (1991a), *West Africa and the Arab World: Historical and Contemporary Perspectives*, Accra: Ghana Academy of Arts and Sciences.

——(1991b), Les Rapports culturelles entre le Maroc et l'Afrique Sub-Saharienne à travers les âges. Rabat: Institut des Etudes Africaines, 1991.

——(1999),Timbuktu and the Songhay Empire; Al-Saʿdī's Taʾrīkh al-Sūdān down to 1613 & other Contemporary Documents, Leiden; Brill. New Edition, 2003.

—— (2006), Jews of a Saharan Oasis: Elimination of the Tamantit Community, Princeton: Markus Wiener Publishers.

——, & Eve Troutt Powell (2002), *The African Diaspora in the Mediterranea Lands of Islam*, Princeton: Markus Wiener.

Ibn ʿAskar, Dawḥat al-nāshir, Fez, 1309/1891–2.

Ibn Baṭṭūṭa (1854)*Voyages d'Ibn Battūta; text arabe accompagné d'une traduction par C Deéfremery et Le Dr. B.R. Sanguinetti*; re-edited by Vincent Monteil, 1968, Paris: Editions Anthropos Paris.

—— (1994), *The Travels of Ibn Baṭṭūṭa*, Vol. IV, trans. H.A.R. Gibb & C. Beckingham, London: Hakluyt Society.

al-\, *Opus Geographicum, sive "Liber ad eorum delectationem qui terras peragrare studeant"*, ed. A.Bombaci, U. Rizzitano, R. Rubinacci, L. Veccia Vaglieri, Naples-Rome, 4 vols. & Index vol., 1970–84,

Kamal, Youssouf (1987), *Monumenta Cartographica Africae et Aegypti*, 6 vols., Frankfurt am Main: Institut ̀fur der Geschichte der Arabisch-Islamischen Wissenschaften an der Johann Wolfgang Goethe-Universĭat.

Kanya-Forstner, A.S. & Lovejoy, Paul (1997), Eds. *Pilgrims, Interpreters and Agents: French Reconnaissance Reports on the Sokoto Caliphate and Borno, 1891–1895* (Madison: African Studies Program, University of Wisconsin.

Kaʿti, Maḥmūd: see TF.

Leo Africanus, *Della discrittione dell'Africa*, trans. by R. Brown, 3 vols., London: Hakluyt Society, 1896; parts trans. in Hunwick (1999), 272–291.

Lewis, I.M. (1965), *The Modern History of Somaliland*, London: Weidenfeld & Nicholson.

O'Fahey, R.S. (1990), *Enigmatic Saint: Ahmad Ibn Idris and the Idrisi Tradition, London: Hurst & Company.*

Saad, Elias N. (1983), *Social History of Timbuktu: the role of Muslim Scholars and Notables, 1400–1900,* Cambridge University Press.

TF—*Taʿrīkh al-Fattāsh* by Maḥmūd Kaʿti.Text and French translation, *Tarikh El-Fettach*, by O. Houdas and M. Delafosse, Paris: Librairie d'Amérique et d'Orient Adrien-Maisonneuve, 1964.

TS—*Taʿrīkh al-Sūdān* by ʿAbd al-Raḥmān al-Saʿdī, with French trans. by O. Houdas, Paris: Librairie d'Amérique et d'Orient Adrien-Maisonneuve, 1964. English trans. in Hunwick (1999).

Usman ∂an Fodio , *Bayān wujūb al-hijra ʿalā ʾl-ʿibād*, with translation by F.H. El Masri , Khartoum University Press & Oxford University Press , 1978 [Fontes Historiae Africanae: Series Arabica, 1].

Umar, Muhammad Sani (2006), *Islam and Colonialism: Intellectual Responses of Muslims of Northern Nigeria to British colonial Rule*, Leiden and Boston: Brill .

Wilks, Ivor (1968), The transmission of Islamic learning in the Western Sudan' in J. Goody (ed.), *Literacy in Traditional Societies*, Cambridge.

Index

Arabic titles, such as *Al-Ḥājj, Mūlāy, Shaykh, Sharīf[a]* and *Qāḍī*, and *al-* 'the', and b. (*ibn* - 'son of) are not dealt with alphabetically; but the names / words they precede are entered in alphabetic order.